Digital Illustration Fundamentals

Wallace Jackson

Apress®

Digital Illustration Fundamentals

Wallace Jackson
Lompoc, California, USA

ISBN-13 (pbk): 978-1-4842-1696-5   ISBN-13 (electronic): 978-1-4842-1697-2
DOI 10.1007/978-1-4842-1697-2

Library of Congress Control Number: 2015958157

Managing Director: Welmoed Spahr
Lead Editor: Steve Anglin
Technical Reviewer: Chád Darby
Editorial Board: Steve Anglin, Louise Corrigan, Jonathan Gennick, Robert Hutchinson,
    Michelle Lowman, James Markham, Susan McDermott, Matthew Moodie, Jeffrey Pepper,
    Douglas Pundick, Ben Renow-Clarke, Gwenan Spearing
Coordinating Editor: Mark Powers
Copy Editor: Karen Jameson
Compositor: SPi Global
Indexer: SPi Global
Artist: SPi Global

Distributed to the book trade worldwide by Springer Science+Business Media New York, 233 Spring Street, 6th Floor, New York, NY 10013. Phone 1-800-SPRINGER, fax (201) 348-4505, e-mail orders-ny@springer-sbm.com, or visit www.springeronline.com. Apress Media, LLC is a California LLC and the sole member (owner) is Springer Science + Business Media Finance Inc (SSBM Finance Inc). SSBM Finance Inc is a **Delaware** corporation.

For information on translations, please e-mail rights@apress.com, or visit www.apress.com.

Apress and friends of ED books may be purchased in bulk for academic, corporate, or promotional use. eBook versions and licenses are also available for most titles. For more information, reference our Special Bulk Sales–eBook Licensing web page at www.apress.com/bulk-sales.

Any source code or other supplementary material referenced by the author in this text is available to readers at www.apress.com/9781484216965. For detailed information about how to locate your book's source code, go to www.apress.com/source-code/. Readers can also access source code at SpringerLink in the Supplementary Material section for each chapter.

Printed on acid-free paper

This book is dedicated to everyone in the open source community who is working so diligently to make professional new media application development software and content development tools freely available to rich application developers so that they can utilize them to achieve our creative dreams and financial goals. Last but not least, I dedicate this book to my father, Parker Jackson; my family; my lifelong friends; and my production ranch neighbors for their constant help, assistance, and those relaxing, late-night BBQs!

Contents at a Glance

Contents

■ CONTENTS

About the Author

Wallace Jackson has been writing for several leading multimedia publications about work in the new media content development industry, after contributing a piece about advanced-computer-processing architectures for the centerfold (a removable "miniissue" insert) of an original issue of *AV Video Multimedia Producer* magazine that wasdistributed at the SIGGRAPH trade show. Wallace has written for alarge number of popular publications about his work in interactive-3D and new-media-advertising campaign design, including *3DArtist* magazine, *Desktop Publisher Journal*, *CrossMedia* magazine, *Kiosk* magazine, *AV VideoMultimedia Producer* magazine, *Digital Signage* magazine, and many other publications.

Wallace has authored a dozen Apress book titles, including four titles in its popular Pro Android series, Java and JavaFX game development titles, digital-image-compositing titles, and new-media-content-production titles.

In the current book on digital image compositing, he focuses on the GIMP and Photoshop CS6 digital-image-compositing software packages, and uses them to demonstrate digital-image-editing and -compositing fundamentals to beginners who wish to become digital imaging professionals.

Wallace is currently the CEO of MindTaffy Design, an agency specializing in new media content production and digital campaign design and development, located in Northern Santa Barbara County, halfway between its clientele in Silicon Valley to the north and Hollywood, the "OC," West LA,and San Diego to the south.

MindTaffy Design has created open source, technology-based (HTML5, JavaScript, Java, JavaFX, and Android 5.3) digital-new-media i3D content deliverables for more than a quarter century (since 1991).

The company's clients consist of a significant number of international branded manufacturers, including Sony, Tyco, Samsung, IBM, Dell, Epson, Nokia, TEAC, Sun Microsystems, Micron, SGI, KDS USA, EIZO, CTX International, KFC, Nanao USA, Techmedia, EZC, and Mitsubishi.

Wallace received his undergraduate BA degree in business economics from the University of California at Los Angeles (UCLA) and his graduate degree in MIS business information systems design and implementation from University of Southern California in Los Angeles (USC). Wallace also received a postgraduate degree in marketing strategy from USC and completed the USC Graduate Entrepreneurship Program. He earned the two USC degrees while at USC's night-time Marshall School of Business MBA Program, which allowed him to work full time as a COBOL programmer while completing his degrees.

About the Technical Reviewer

Chád ("Shod") Darby is an author, instructor, and speaker in the Java development world. As a recognized authority on Java applications and architectures, he has presented technical sessions at software development conferences worldwide (in the United States, UK, India, Russia, and Australia). In his fifteen years as a professional software architect, he's had the opportunity to work for Blue Cross/Blue Shield, Merck, Boeing, Red Hat, and a handful of startup companies.

Chád is a contributing author to several Java books, including *Professional Java E-Commerce* (Wrox Press), *Beginning Java Networking* (Wrox Press), and *XML and Web Services Unleashed* (Sams Publishing). Chád has Java certifications from Sun Microsystems and IBM. He holds a BS in computer science from Carnegie Mellon University.

You can visit Chád's blog at www.luv2code.com to view his free video tutorials on Java. You can also follow him on Twitter at @darbyluvs2code.

Acknowledgments

I would like to acknowledge all my fantastic editors and their support staff at Apress, who worked those long hours and toiled so very hard on this book to make it the ultimate image-compositing-fundamentals book title currently on the market.

I thank:

Steve Anglin for his work as the Acquisitions Editor for the book and for recruiting me to write development titles at Apress covering widely popular open source content development platforms (Android, Java, JavaFX, HTML5, CSS3, JS, GIMP, etc.).

Matthew Moodie for his work as the Development Editor on the book and for his experience and guidance during the process of making the book one of the leading digital illustration titles.

Mark Powers for his work as the Coordinating Editor for the book and for his constant diligence in making sure that I either hit my chapter delivery deadlines or far surpassed them.

Karen Jameson for her work as the Copy Editor on this book, for her careful attention to minute details, and for conforming the text to current Apress book writing standards.

Chád Darby for his work as the Technical Reviewer on the book and for making sure that I didn't make technical mistakes.

CHAPTER 1

■ ■ ■

The Foundation of Digital Illustration: Points and Lines

Welcome to *Digital Illustration Fundamentals*! This book will take you through the foundation of digital illustration, as well as covering how to use vector illustration assets with popular computer programming languages and open source content publishing platforms such as Kindle, Android Studio, HTML5, and JavaFX. I will start at the lowest level concepts – in this chapter it is the **vertex** and the lines that connect these vertices together – and then we will build upon each of these foundational concepts in subsequent chapters, until you have a comprehensive understanding of digital illustration modeling, color, gradient or pattern shading, command editing and vector rendering concepts and associated terminology, file formats, work flows, spline editing, effects processing, data footprint optimization, computer programming, and content publishing.

I will show you how these concepts, techniques, and terms apply to the Inkscape open source digital illustration software package. This just so happens to be free for commercial use and very similar in features to Adobe Illustrator and CorelDRAW.

For this reason, part of the chapter, logically the first part, would be how to download and install open source Inkscape software, just in case you do not have any digital illustration software on your multimedia workstation currently. Then, you'll learn about the foundational elements of digital illustration.

Industry professionals call this a "vertex" or a "node." Once you put this together with other "vertices," the new media result comprises what's called a vector "shape."

How these digital illustration vector shapes are created and rendered is what this book is all about, and we will build on the knowledge in this chapter with curves, fills, gradients, patterns, commands, algorithms, tracing, layers, editing tools, fonts, data footprint optimization, content delivery, and more, until you understand everything about this digital illustration work process and how it can be used with modern-day devices.

Downloading and Installing Inkscape

All our readers are going to need to have digital illustration software of one type or another, whether that is CorelDRAW or Adobe Illustrator or Macromedia Freehand. If you do not own any of these, you can use the free-for-commercial-use **Inkscape**. Let's install Inkscape for Windows, Mac OS X, or Linux, next.

© Wallace Jackson 2015
W. Jackson, *Digital Illustration Fundamentals*, DOI 10.1007/978-1-4842-1697-2_1

1

Inkscape.org: Get Inkscape Illustration Software

To download the current stable version of Inkscape, you will go to: **http://www. inkscape.org**, and click on the green **Download Arrow** link, seen in Figure 1-1, or alternately click on the **Download** tab, which is directly underneath the Inkscape logo.

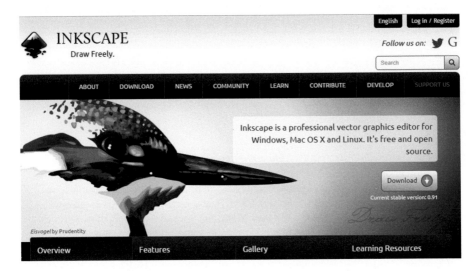

Figure 1-1. *Go to the inkscape.org, and click the Download arrow*

Download the **inkscape-0.91-x64.msi** installer file if you are using Windows or a Linux or Mac version. Next, right-click on it and select the Install option to start your installation process. Inkscape for Windows uses a 64-bit version, since most modern-day workstations run 64-bit Windows Vista, 7, 8.1, or 10. Figure 1-2 shows the downloaded file, which has been selected, and right-clicked on to reveal the context-sensitive menu, with this **Install** option selected in blue. If for some reason you do not own a 64-bit content production workstation, go to Walmart, and purchase a brand name workstation tower for $400 to $500. I have used, and recommend, the Acer, HP, and Compaq workstations.

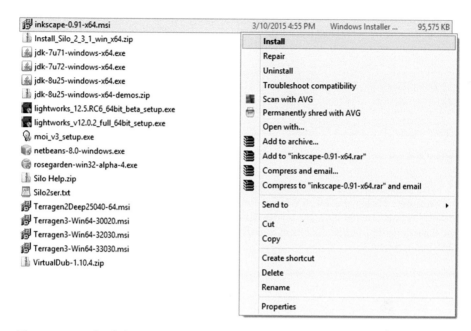

Figure 1-2. *Right-click on .MSI file, and select Install option*

Once your installation starts, click the NEXT button, as is shown on the left-hand side of Figure 1-2.

Once you click on the Next button you'll get an **End-User License Agreement** dialog. Select the I accept the terms in the License Agreement check box, and then click on **Next** to continue.

Next click on the **Typical** installation type button, then click on the **Next** button, as is shown on the right-hand side in Figure 1-3.

Figure 1-3. *Click Install, then Next, then the Typical Button*

This will give you the **Ready to Install Inkscape** dialog, seen in Figure 1-4 on the left, where you can click on **Install**.

Figure 1-4. *Accept default installation options, and click Next*

You will then get your **Installing Inkscape** progress bar, and once that has finished, the **Completed Inkscape Setup Wizard** dialog will appear. Click the Finish button, and install shortcut icons to Inkscape on the desktop or taskbar for easy launch access. Once you have done this, launch Inkscape, and make sure that it works. You should see what is shown in Figure 1-5.

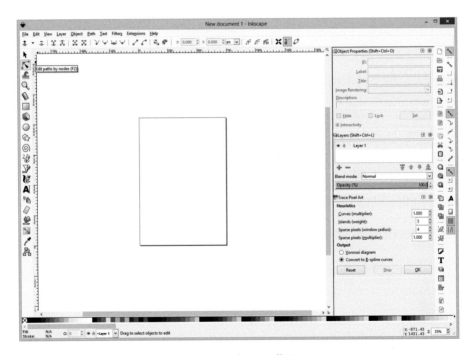

Figure 1-5. *Click the Install Button to begin the installation*

Now let's take a look at some of the basic elements of a vector illustration asset, called vertices, paths, and lines.

Basic Vector Shapes: Vertices and Lines

Digital illustration vector imagery is composed of shape objects that are composed of "data points," called "vertices"; or in Inkscape, "nodes," which are placed in 2D space, by using **X,Y coordinates**. Lines, arcs, or curves then connect the **vertex** points together. We will be looking at concepts and terminology for these points and lines during this section. If you create a "closed" shape, that is, one where there are no openings for a fill (color, pattern, or gradient) to escape, you can also fill a vector shape so that the shape looks solid instead of empty. In fact, you can fill your open shape, but the fill will act as though the shape were closed, so this is not generally done.

The Vertex: A Foundation for 2D and 3D Geometry

The foundation for any 2D (or 3D) vector geometry asset is called the vertex. Multiple **vertices** (the plural of vertex) are required to create a **line** or **arc**, which require two vertices, or a **closed shape**, which requires at least three vertices if you are using lines, or two vertices if you are using arcs or curves. Vertices are used in 2D vector (SVG) data processing, as well as in 3D vector (OpenGL) data processing, both of which are integrated into Java, JavaFX, HTML5, and Android Studio.

   Vertex data is outlined in SVG using X,Y coordinates, as mentioned earlier, which tell the processor where the vertex is located in 2D space. Without these vertex coordinates, lines and curves cannot be drawn, as they must have an **origin**, as well as a **destination** vertex coordinate, as part of vector line drawing operations. A line or arc would be an example of an **open shape**.

   When we get into creating and looking at **SVG data** you'll notice that these X,Y numeric pairs are the majority of the SVG data, which can be contained using the XML format, or in a Java SVG object for Android Studio application. SVG data can also be used in your JavaScript (HTML5) code as well as in JavaFX (Java 8 or Java 9) code, so it is compatible across each of your open platform new media application or content development workflow.

   An X,Y coordinate, all by its lonesome, is what's termed **one dimensional** or **1D**. You'll need two vertex coordinates to be considered to be two dimensional, or 2D; so, a line or a curve, that is, an open shape or a closed shape, will be a 2D object.

   Next, let's take a look at the next level up from the 1D vertex shape element, the 2D **path** vector shape element. This 2D path data comprises the majority of a **scalable vector graphics**, or SVG, shape definition, which can be defined using XML, Java, JavaFX, Android Studio, HTML5, or JavaScript.

The Path: Connect the Vertices to Create a Shape

Your path is defined in SVG using a "path data" element. Both an open shape, as well as a closed shape, are technically paths, according to the open source SVG specification. This SVG Path represents the outline of an open or closed shape that can be **filled**, **stroked**, or even used as a **clipping** path. We will be covering these concepts in detail during the book, but briefly, a fill deals with the interior of a path, strokes deal with the line or curve thickness that styles your path, and the clipping path is used for Boolean operations or cutting interiors out.

In SVG data an SVG Path object represents 2D "geometry," used to outline a Path object. In fact, in JavaFX, the class is actually called the **SVGPath** class. SVG path data can be defined in terms of **SVG commands,** which I'll cover in a later chapter in the book. Briefly, some of them include a **moveto** command, which sets your current point; a **lineto** command, which draws straight lines; and a **curveto** command, which draws a cubic Bézier curve. A **closepath** command can be used to close an open shape, drawing a closing line to the shapes starting point. If you try to fill an open shape, this closepath command will be used by the fill, but without drawing a visible line boundary for that portion of the shape, which you will see in Chapter 3, covering stroke and fill operations.

Compound paths are also possible in SVG; these allow you to create complex, Boolean shape special effects. For instance, you could use a compound path to create a hole in your shape.

Straight Lines: Inkscape's Pencil Freehand Drawing Tool

The simplest way to connect the **vertex coordinates** along any path is to utilize **straight lines**. Different shapes such as triangles, rectangles, pentagons, hexagons, and octagons will be created by using the lineto command.

There are three lineto commands: a lineto, a horizontal lineto, and a vertical lineto. We'll be looking at SVG commands in detail during Chapter 6.

To draw a line in Inkscape you would use the Pencil tool as shown selected (in blue) on the left side of Figure 1-6. The Pencil (Freehand) tool allows you to draw straight lines.

To use this tool, click once where you want the line to begin, and a second time where you want the line to end.

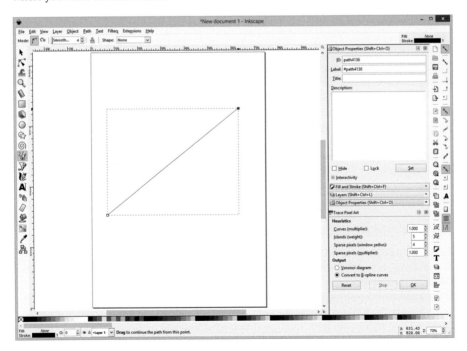

Figure 1-6. *Use the Freehand (Pencil icon) tool to draw a line*

Next let's take a look at the elliptical arc, which is a simple curve by nature with a complex set of specification data for its SVG command, which is why, for my programming projects, I will usually stick with either a Cubic or a Quadratic Bézier curve, from a shape modeling perspective, as you will soon see during Chapter 2 on modeling curves using Inkscape.

Elliptical Arcs: Inkscape's Circles, Ellipses, and Arcs Tool

One of the three types of SVG curve commands is the elliptical arc, which uses a capital A (absolute arc) or lower-case a (relative arc) as you will see in Chapter 6. We will also cover some of the arc-related content here, as well as take a look at how the Circles, Ellipses, and Arcs tool works in Inkscape. Open Inkscape and click the solid circle in the toolbar on the left side of the software, as shown in Figure 1-7. At the top of the software on the left are the options and option icons for each of the Inkscape primary tools, which are aligned vertically on the left of the software package, as you have seen already in Figures 1-5 through 1-7. Click underneath the straight line you just drew and draw out an oval (ellipse) shape on your screen.

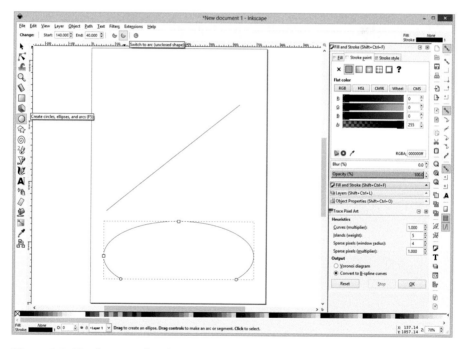

Figure 1-7. *Use the Arc tool and top icons to specify open arc*

In your **Fill tab** on the right, click the **X** (no fill); and in the **Stroke Paint tab**, click the **stroked square**, and keep the default setting of a **black one pixel** stroke. At the top left of Inkscape, set a **140** degree **Start** and **40** degree **End** setting, and click the **Open (unclosed) Shape icon**, as shown in Figure 1-7.

This will give you the open arc, much like you would get if you used your SVG command language to draw this shape. Let's take a look at that now, just so that you have a concept of how this works. We'll get into commands in detail during Chapter 7.

The SVG arc command draws the segment of an ellipse. Arc takes the largest number of parameters of any of your SVG curve drawing related commands, and takes the following basic format:

```
M x,y A radius-x,radius-y x-axis-rotation large-arc-flag sweep-flag x,y
```

Here, **M** (moveto) x,y is your **starting point** for the arc, radius-x is the x-radius for an ellipse, radius-y is a y-radius for an ellipse, x-axis-rotation is a number of rotation degrees to rotate your x-axis, two on/off flags for large/small arc and sweep/no-sweep arc, and the final x,y coordinates are your end point for this arc.

It is important to note that setting both x and y radius (the rx and ry values) to identical values will create a circle instead of an ellipse, as this setting equality will makes your curvature symmetrical.

The elliptical arc has a number of parameters, including a coordinate pair, the size of the ellipse being described, the angle, and two flags that alter the rendering.

The example will also allow you to modify whether an arc coordinates are absolute (A), or relative (a), to your starting point (defined by the red circle).

An example can be seen in Figure 1-8, which shows the following Elliptical Arc SVG command:

```
M 125,300 A 225,100 0 1 1 375,300
```

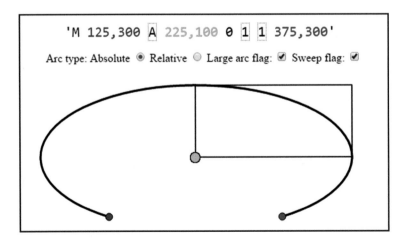

Figure 1-8. *Elliptical Arc with Sweep and Large Arc Flags*

8

If you instead wanted the missing segment for this ellipse at the bottom, you would deselect, or set to zero, the large arc flag and the sweep flag, which would draw the smaller part of the arc and mirror it around an X-axis. The SVG command for this would look something like the following sequence:

```
M 125,300 A 225,100 0 0 0 375,300
```

As you can see, the radius-x, radius-y parameters create different angles that distort the ellipse from being a circle into an elliptical shape.

If this interests you, there are a number of these SVG curve generators on the Internet, if you wanted to experiment with these parameters further.

Summary

In this first chapter, I made sure that you had a digital illustration software package installed and ready to master, as well as taking a look at the foundational elements of digital illustration, also known as 2D vector illustration. These included the **vertex**, the **path**, the **line**, and the **arc**. Since we have a lot to cover in this book, I wanted to cover several of these basic concepts, and at least one set of shapes (circles, ellipses, and arcs) during this first chapter.

In the next chapter, you will take a look at a much more complex version of the line, known as the **Bézier curve**, and how to create these advanced curves in Inkscape.

CHAPTER 2

■ ■ ■

The Curvature of Digital Illustration: Spline Curves

Now that we have installed Inkscape and covered some of those low-level 2D vector illustration concepts, including vertices; and the straight lines that can connect these vertices together to form polygons; and the algorithmically generated circles, ellipses, and arcs, we can get into the more complex Bézier spline curves that are the mainstay of both 2D and 3D geometry modeling pipelines (work processes).

We'll discuss different types of Bézier curves supported in SVG and then learn how to use your new Inkscape illustration software to create a complex, custom shape using Bézier curves. I'll continue to cover the basic SVG command structures for the shape components that I cover in each chapter, so we have fewer topics that we need to have in Chapter 7 covering SVG Commands.

Custom Shapes: Intro to Bézier Curves

Most of the complex, custom 2D shape geometry you are going to be creating will use the Bézier curve, as advanced illustration projects seldom are built on simple vector geometry shapes such as circles, ovals, pentagons, octagons, or even complex shapes, such as text fonts or clip art that have been modeled for you. At some point in time you are going to want to create your own custom 2D geometric shapes, and that's why we're going to learn about Bézier curves during this chapter. We'll create a complex 2D vector shape using only a few vertices (also called nodes or data points). This is highly optimized data, as you will see in Chapter 7, when we turn these 2D vector geometry creations into mathematical data that you can use in HTML5, XML, Java, JavaFX, JavaScript, and similar mark-up and programming languages. These are used in popular, open source, content publishing platforms, including Google's Android Studio and Chrome OS, Mozilla's Firefox OS, Opera OS, Canonical's Ubuntu Touch OS, Tizen OS, Amazon's Kindle, Fire OS and Fire TV, EPUB 3, and Adobe's PDF.

© Wallace Jackson 2015
W. Jackson, *Digital Illustration Fundamentals*, DOI 10.1007/978-1-4842-1697-2_2

Cubic Bézier Curve: Two Control Point Spline

If you have ever used the Pen tool in Photoshop or GIMP, or any of the 3D modeling tools out there such as Blender, then you are probably familiar with the **Cubic Bézier** curve. I am not going to go into all of the detail behind how Bézier curves are constructed mathematically, as this is a fundamentals book, and not an advanced book, but we will be looking at how to use open source software tools to generate digital illustration vector assets you will need for your multimedia content applications.

You can also draw these Cubic Bézier curves by using SVG command structures. This is done by defining your **start** and **end** vertex, as well as two **control points**. One control point is for your start point, and one control point is for your end point.

The control points are used to "control"; I like to call this **conform**, the curvature of a curve, also called a **spline** in the industry. The curvature of a spline will be conformed going away from the first vertex by its control point and coming into the second vertex using the second control point. You should be able to visualize this concept more clearly, in the second part of this chapter, when you start to model using Cubic Bézier curves with your new open source Inkscape vector illustration package.

This Cubic Bézier curve should utilize the following SVG command structure (data format):

```
M x,y  C (or c) x1,y1 x2,y2 x,y
```

The **starting point** is defined by **moveto** M x,y, and the **C** (or c) defines an absolute or relative Cubic Bézier **curve** type. The x1,y1 is your control point for the beginning of the curve, and the x2,y2 is your control point for the end of curve. Finally, your x,y coordinate at the end of the command string is an **end point** for the Cubic Bézier curve.

Next let's take a look at the other type of Bézier curve that is supported in the scalable vector graphics (SVG) format, the **Quadratic Bézier** curve.

Quadratic Bézier Curve: One Control Point Spline

Your inclination will be to assume that Quadratic Bézier curves may be more complicated, given that quad means four, and therefore, that there are two more control points for this type of curve. The exact opposite of this assumption is actually the case, because a Quadratic Bézier curve actually has only single control point control! This **single control point** connects with both the start point and end point of the curve segment. Moving this single control point controls how your curve is conformed between your two vertices (your start and end data points).

Therefore if you were looking for a way to implement any data footprint optimization work process for your illustrations (vector imagery), one way to do accomplish is by SVG coordinate data reduction. Reducing the control points in complex 2D model data represents a 100% data reduction as far as a control point specification is concerned. To accomplish this optimization you would therefore want to utilize these Quadratic Bézier curves.

Your SVG command specification for this Quadratic Bézier curve will therefore appear simpler, using the following data:

```
M x,y  Q (or q) x1,y1 x,y
```

So the Quadratic Bézier command requires only one single control point, which is then used as the control point for both start and end points. So, it's like the two control points in a Cubic Bézier curve are connected together as one control point, which moves the curvature from the start point and into the end point at the same time. There are numerous SVG curve generators on the Internet, if you want to experiment with the parameters.

Using Splines: Creating Complex Shapes

Now that you have played around with one of Inkscape's basic shape tools, the circles, ellipses and arcs tool, let's get down to more serious **2D geometry modeling**, and focus on drawing Bézier splines in this chapter. Bézier splines are also used in 3D modeling as well, so you'll get used to using them in the 2D Inkscape vector software package, and then graduate to Blender later on if you want to take your skills into three dimensions. Besides, most of what you will be creating for your multimedia applications would be made either out of 3D polygons, 3D NURBS, or 2D (or 3D) Bézier Splines, so it's practical for us to focus on these Cubic Bézier spline tools in Inkscape and learn how to use these tools for shape creation and optimization work flows.

The Draw Bézier Curves Tool: 2D Shape Modeling

Start a **New Project** in Inkscape, using a **File ➤ New** menu sequence, and select your **Draw Bézier curves and straight lines** tool. This is seen on the left side of the screen in Figure 2-1 about halfway down on the Inkscape toolbar. I left the tool-tip pop-up mouse-over help comment visible so that you could see it more easily. You should mouse-over tool icons, as well as other user interface elements, to see what they do. You can learn a lot simply by using this handy pop-up tool-tip functionality. Next, let's create a complex Bézier spline shape such as a heart, and only use four data points to do this since this is a chapter on optimization.

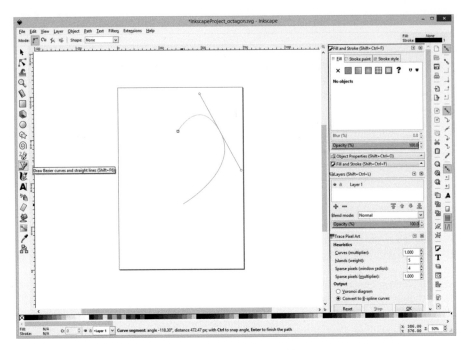

Figure 2-1. *Click start point, click to right, pull out handles*

As I mentioned, the way to optimize vector illustrations is to place fewer vertex data points, and fewer control points, which are represented in Inkscape as **spline tensioning handles**.

To create your heart in Inkscape, select the Draw Bézier curves and straight lines tool, and click in the center of your page about 25% of the way down from the top. The starting point in Inkscape is shown using a hollow square point called a **node**.

The Draw Bézier curve icon shows a pen tip drawing out a spline curve, while pulling a spline tensioning control handle, out of one of the spline curve's nodes (also called a vertex or data point). Once you click on this icon, your cursor will turn into a **fountain pen**, and you can then begin to place your first vertex, which is shown as a hollow, square node, in Figure 2-1.

Click a second point to the right of this starting point close to the page's right side. This is shown where blue spline tensioning handles meet and the green curve segment one and red current curve segment (two) also meet, as shown in Figure 2-1.

Pull the spline handles out from the second point as you click (and drag) it, to create a rough curvature approximation.

You will fine-tune this later on, so it does not have to be perfect right off the bat. Once you've let go (released your mouse-down operation, to stop drag-handles mode), you will move the spline down, toward where you want the tip of your heart.

Next, click on the point that will be your bottom point for this heart shape, which should be directly underneath your start point, and about 60% of the way from the top of the page, or 40% of the way from the bottom of the page.

14

Draw your third segment of the heart curve up to a point that is the opposite, or mirror image of, the second point, on the left side of your starting point this time. This should be about the same distance from the left edge of the page as your second point was from the right side of your page, as shown in Figure 2-2. Click your third point to the left of the starting point, close to the page's left side. This is shown where blue spline tensioning handles meet, and green curve segment three, and red current curve segment four meet, as seen in Figure 2-2.

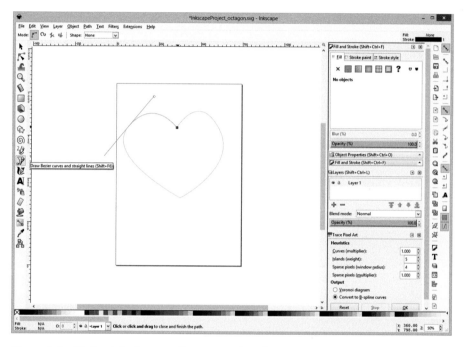

Figure 2-2. *Click to left of start, adjust tension handles, then place end point for heart over start point (turns red)*

Again pull your spline handles out from the third point, as you click, and drag the spline tensioning handles, to create your rough curve approximation for the left top of your heart.

Once you have let go and released the mouse-down to stop the drag tensioning handles mode, you can move the fourth curve segment end point, to a final destination over the start point.

If you connect an end point to a starting point for any shape (path) you are creating, it will make that shape **closed**.

In Inkscape, if you position an end point of a path draw operation over your starting point for the path draw operation, the mutual point will turn **red**, as seen in Figure 2-2. Once the point turns red, you can then click, and close your heart path.

Once you click on your start point, your fifth end point and your start point become the same (start) point, so you have used only four points and only four curve segments to create an optimized closed heart shape path. Very Impressive, my Readers!

Once you close the shape the green and red segment color guides will disappear, and your entire Bézier spline curve will be colored black, and be one pixel in thickness. Note this will simply show you where your Bézier curve path is, because a path actually has no thickness. Mathematically speaking, the path is infinitely thin and has no volume until you stroke it, which we will cover during Chapter 3. As you can see in Figure 2-3, your left side of the heart came out better than the right side did.

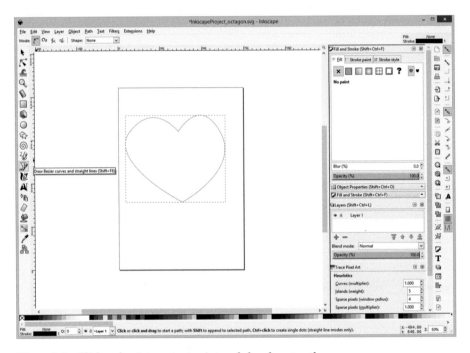

Figure 2-3. *Click end point on start point and close heart path*

For this next section of the chapter, we will be looking at how to edit these spline curve constructs in Inkscape.

Editing a path is done with a different tool in Inkscape called the **Edit path by nodes** tool. This is provided so that an artist can go back and fine-tune node (control point or vertex) handles, or so vector artists can further edit existing paths.

Notice that there are many different terms used for your spline tensioning handle points (control points), and vertices, nodes, points, or coordinates (data points) that make up a path comprised of Bézier spline curves. Next, we'll refine the heart and improve its path shape, using the Edit Paths by Nodes tool. This is one of those often-used tools in Inscape, as indicated by its location right underneath the Arrow (or Selection) tool.

The Edit Paths by Nodes Tool: Refining 2D Shapes

The tool icon for an Edit Path Tool (for short) shows an acute triangle node selector cursor selecting nodes for editing with spline tensioning handles telescoping out of a node. Once you select this tool, your heart shape will show nodes (points, or vertices) that are between Bézier curve segments, as hollow points. This tool is shown selected (in blue) in Figure 2-4.

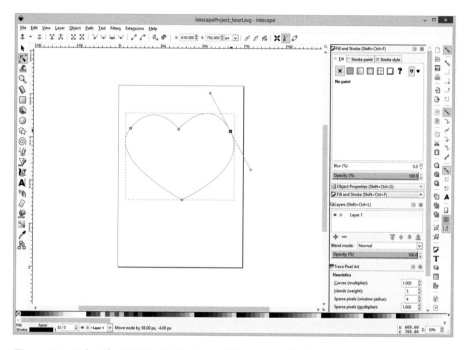

Figure 2-4. *Select the Edit Paths Tool and click on second node*

Let's start by selecting the second node, located at the right side of the heart. Once you click on this node and select it, it will turn red, and spline tensioning handles will emerge from the node, as shown on the right-hand side of Figure 2-5.

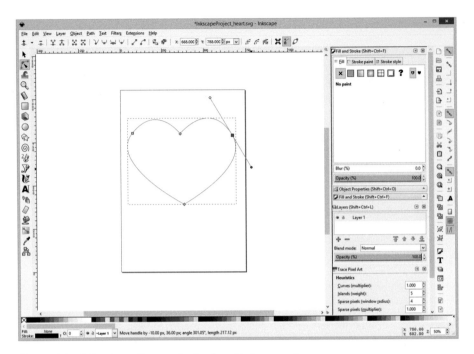

Figure 2-5. *Adjusting spline tensioning handle for second curve*

The spline tensioning handles control curvatures for two different curve segments, one on each side of the node. The top handle, moved using the little circle at the end of the handle, which turns red when it in use, controls the curvature of where your line segment one comes into vertex number two.

The bottom handle, also moved with the circle at the end of the handle, controls the curvature of where line segment two is coming out of vertex number two, and is seen as red (in use) in Figure 2-5, as I adjust the bottom part of the curvature.

Moving the spline handle end point will change the angle of the handle, and affect the curvature of your curve, which is attached to the vertex and defined with that vertex. The length of a spline tensioning handle defines how curved, or straight, the spline is, going into the handle. To create square corners, put that point at the end of your handle on top of its vertex.

If you shorten or lengthen the handles by moving the end points closer to (or farther from) the vertex itself, the curve will become more curved by using longer handles, or less curved by using shorter spline tensioning handles.

If you put your handle points on top of, or retract them back into, the vertex, it will then become a corner point, and the curve coming out of the point will become a line (polygon).

There are also different keyboard modifiers that turn on angle snap (Control), lock your curvature (Alternate) or handle length, and break the handle symmetry, coming out of the vertex or node (Shift). This is a tool that you will need to practice using for some length of time, in order to become proficient or professional in its usage. Be sure to explore the Edit Paths by Node Tool option toolbar, at the top left of Inkscape, as well.

The first thing we need to fix, in a currently imperfect heart path, is the bulbous right side. To fix this curvature we will need to adjust the curve coming out of your second vertex, which will be done by using the lower segment of the tensioning handle, which is shown (along with this heart defect) in Figure 2-5, and which is shown, once it has been fixed, in Figure 2-6.

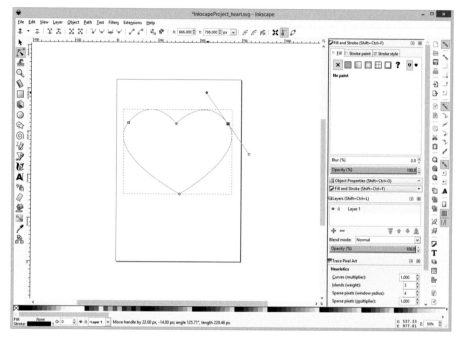

Figure 2-6. *Adjust top tensioning handle to make shape rounder*

If you want to follow along with the heart surgery we're doing in Inkscape, you can open your **InkscapeProject_heart.svg** file series, which can be found in the repository for the book.

To reduce the ballooning of this curve at the right side of the heart, pull the end point of your lower handle closer to the curve of the heart until the second curve of the four heart curves becomes symmetrical to the third curve of the four heart curves, as is shown in Figure 2-6.

Using the Edit Paths by Nodes tool requires what's often called "tweaking," which means making slight adjustments to the vertices and their tensioning handles more than one time around so as to gradually refine a shape; in this case, it is a heart.

Now that the bottom part (curve) of vertex number two is adjusted, let's work on the top part, that is, the curve coming into vertex number two.

As you can see in Figure 2-5, the rounded portion of the top part of the heart on the right half of the heart is square, or squarish, and needs to be more rounded like the left half.

As you can see in Figure 2-6, I have shortened this top part of the spline tensioning handle by around 15%, to make the curvature match the other (left) side of the heart shape better again by reducing an amount of curvature coming into the second vertex.

Now that the top half of the heart is improved we should now start to tweak the center points on the top and the bottom, to continue to refine this heart shape even more.

Pull the bottom vertex down to refine the height of your heart, as shown in Figure 2-7. Since the tip of this heart does not have any round curves (it is sharp), this means that spline tensioning handles are currently located directly on top of the third vertex, so essentially, they are "hidden."

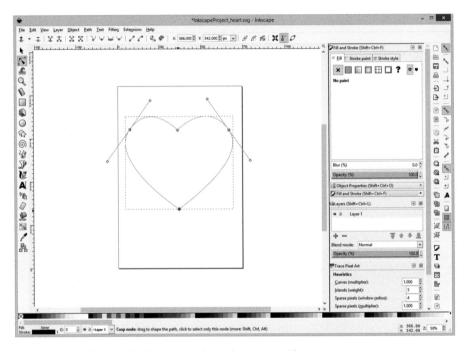

Figure 2-7. *Pull down the bottom vertex and center it with top*

If you want to stylize the bottom of the heart, hold the **Shift** key down and pull the spline tensioning handle out of the vertex. I show this in Figure 2-9, so you can see what I mean.

To do this, place your cursor over the bottom vertex, so it turns red, and then depress the Shift key (and hold it down) and click and drag in any direction, to pull the spline tension handle out of the node (vertex).

You can also pull down the top point, vertex #1, as seen in Figure 2-8, if you like, which will provide more pronounced curvature in the top of your heart shape.

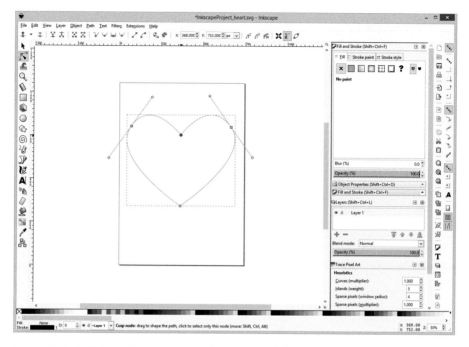

Figure 2-8. *Pull down the top vertex and center it with bottom*

This will serve to enhance the curvature on each side at the top of your heart, making your heart shape more pronounced.

Once you refine this dip at the top middle of the heart, you will need to refine the spline tensioning handles at vertex #2 and vertex #4 again. This is a part of the iterative process that is called **tweaking**.

Yes, I know, there are other things, which are described using this exact same term, which are not nearly as productive, as making iterative spline tension handle adjustments can be.

At this point in the tweaking process, the heart's shape is just a matter of taste, so continue to tweak the four Bézier curve vertices, and their spline tension handle control points, until you have that final, end result that you desire, for your sweetheart on Valentine's Day.

If you wanted to stylize this tip of your heart, located at the bottom of the shape at vertex number three, you can drag the tensioning handles back out of the sharp corner, as is seen in Figure 2-9, by holding down the Shift keyboard modifier, and clicking on a selected vertex and dragging your mouse away from the selected (red) control point (node or vertex).

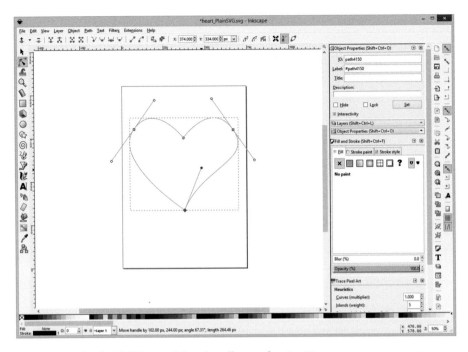

Figure 2-9. *Use the Shift key and drag handle out of vertex #3*

This will pull spline tensioning handles out of the node so that you can introduce curvature into this area of the heart as seen in Figure 2-9. I this case, we are going to make what I call a "negative curve" where the curve goes in rather than out to give the bottom part of the heart more style and character.

Again, as you can see in Figure 2-9 on the right, you'll need to tweak your spline tensioning handles for vertex #2, to make the top right part of your heart have a thicker (positive) curvature.

As you can see in Figure 2-10, this same exact curvature effect happens on the left side of the heart, when I introduced this styling in a symmetric fashion.

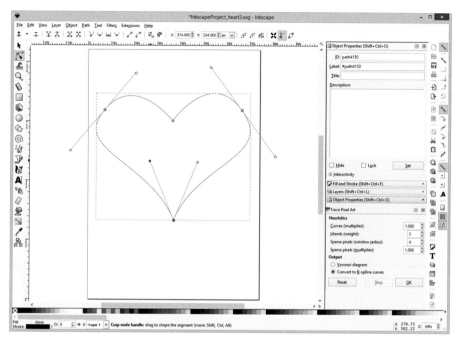

Figure 2-10. *Use Shift key, drag another handle out of vertex 3*

To get some practice working with these tools, adjust #2 and #4 vertices spline tensioning handles to make the top round areas of the heart more round, and less squarish, as shown in Figure 2-10, unless, of course, you like this heart stylization effect. Notice if you positioned the vertex #2 and vertex #4 in mirrored positions to each other that you could also mirror the curvature, by mirroring the spline tensioning handle length and positioning. Play around this concept as well, using your heart model, as it clearly has some symmetry to it.

If you really want to master these spline modeling tools you will need to experiment, practice, and refine your skills.

Learn what all the option icons, located at the top left of Inkscape, do for your Bézier Path tool. The left two insert and delete nodes, the next four join or break path or segments between nodes, the next four apply algorithms to spline tension handles, and the last four apply conversion algorithms to shape constructs. You can find out what each of these does, simply by positioning your mouse cursor over each configuration icon, and then reading the pop-up tool-tip helper text to see what it does.

Learn the keystroke modifiers for each icon, so that you can speed the work process and become a 2D spline modeler star.

I've seen modelers at trade shows, such as SIGGRAPH, who can spline model objects in minutes, leaving massive crowds of people aghast at their impressive spline modeling skill levels.

Now you could make a professional career out of modeling 2D clip art assets, if you like. Once of the great things about splines, and the way Inkscape is set up, is that you can refine your shapes for as long as you want to, until they are perfect.

Summary

In this second chapter, we took a closer look at some of the more complex elements of 2D modeling for your digital illustration workflow, also known as 2D vector illustration. These included the **Cubic Bézier** spline and the **Quadratic Bézier** spline. We also looked at how to use Inkscape to model a fairly complex shape, a highly stylized heart, using only four vertex elements and four Cubic Bézier spline curves.

In the next chapter, you will take a look at **Strokes and Fills**, and how to create shape geometry styling features, using Inkscape.

CHAPTER 3

■ ■ ■

The Styling of Digital Illustration: Stroke and Fill

Now that we have covered some of the low-level 2D vector illustration concepts, including vertices, straight lines, and Bézier curves that can connect these vertices together, as well as the algorithmically generated circles, ellipses, and arcs, we can take a look at some other shape generation tools that are supported in Inkscape. We will also take a look at the Inkscape user interface in greater detail during the first part of this chapter, since it is something that we need to cover before we get too far into the book.

As a part of looking at some of these other vector shape tools, you'll also learn about stroking and filling operations, which is what this chapter is primarily about. I'll continue to cover the basic SVG command structures for the shape components that I cover in this chapter, so there are fewer topics that we need to have in Chapter 7, covering SVG Commands.

Industry professionals call this "geometry decoration" a number of different terms. In Android and HTML5, this is called "styling," in 3D, it is called "shading" or "texturing," and in UI design it is called "skinning." Once you put this decoration that we are going to cover in the chapter (stroke and fill) and in Chapter 4 (patterns and gradients), together with your shape definition data, you will have the ability to create impressive 2D vector digital illustration assets.

Inkscape: Vector Illustration Shape Styles

Since vector media assets are inherently data optimized, as long as you use the smallest number of vertices (points and their data coordinates) possible to create your 2D assets, with the correct type of Bézier splines for your modeling objective, we will focus during this chapter on how to use Inkscape to create these 2D vector assets.

Later during Chapter 7 we will look at how to use Export functions to turn these into SVG commands using XML markup that you can utilize not only in Android Studio, but also in JavaFX, and in HTML5, primarily by properly using CSS3 and JavaScript.

© Wallace Jackson 2015
W. Jackson, *Digital Illustration Fundamentals*, DOI 10.1007/978-1-4842-1697-2_3

The UI Layout: Overview of Key Areas in Inkscape

The Inkscape user interface can be very complex, as this software gives you virtually everything you'll need for your 2D vector illustration new media asset content creation workflow. In a nutshell, there are three vertical toolbars: your primary **functional tools** on the left, your **snap-to** settings on the far right, and your **command tools** on the inside right toolbar seen in Figure 3-1. There is a **floating palette docking** area on the right of your **canvas**, that white page in the center of your UI.

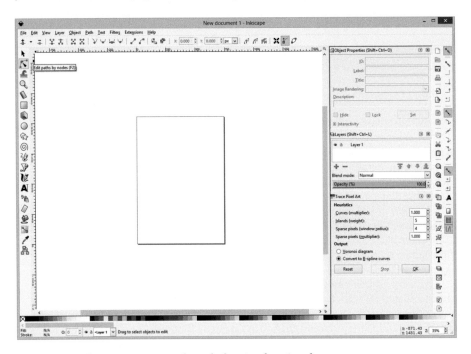

Figure 3-1. Inkscape on program launch showing functional areas

At the very top are **drop-down menus**, and underneath that is your horizontal toolbar, containing **options** for the selected tool. At the bottom of the UI is your **color swatch selector** for shape fills and strokes. At the very bottom is a **status bar** for numeric representation of active shapes and work flow settings.

Let's get right into learning how to use the other shape creation tools in Inkscape that we have not covered thus far.

Polygon Shapes: Creating Basic Closed Shapes

Polygon shapes are more commonly found in i3D vector new media. Polygons are 2D shapes, which have straight lines around their perimeter. Some examples would include the following: triangles, rectangles, squares, and shapes such as pentagons, hexagons, and octagons. Let's use the Inkscape **Create stars and polygons** tool, shown in Figure 3-2, and create a basic green octagon polygon first.

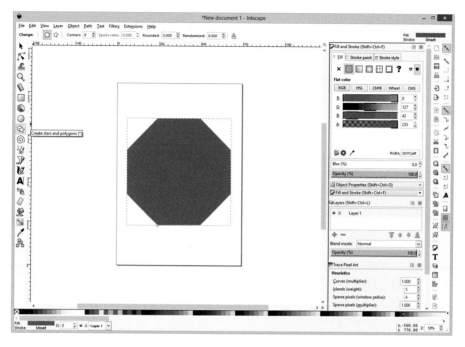

Figure 3-2. *Create a green octagon with stars and polygons tool*

Use the Create stars and polygons tool shown selected in Figure 3-2 and select the **polygon** option at the top left in the options toolbar, shown in blue (selected).

Set the **Corners** spinner to **8** then click in the middle of the page, and pull out the octagon shape.

You can not only control the size of this polygon, when you pull it out from the center, but also its rotation. I made the sides align with the top, bottom, and sides of the canvas.

Next, let's take a look at how to fill your octagon with a green color, using Inkscape's floating palette docking area.

Solid Color Fill: Using Fill to Color Your Octagon Dark Green

You will then use the Fill and Stroke palette, seen on the top right in Figure 3-2. Select the **Fill** tab and then set the **Flat color** to use **RGB** color. Set the **Green** slider to a 50% value of **127** and set the **Blue** slider to a 16% value of **42**. Click a **solid color icon** (second from the left) to specify a solid color for your fill. We will be looking at the other icons in Chapter 4, when we cover gradients and patterns. If the Fill and Stroke palette is not visible, you can open it using the **Object ➤ Fill and Stroke** menu or by clicking the (closed) Fill and Stroke bar in the palette docking area at the right side of the software.

As you can see in Figure 3-2 the interior of the octagon polygon is now filled with a nice solid green color, just as we instructed it to. Solid color fills are the easiest to define, as all you have to do is select a color mode and color settings in order to specify a color that you want to see inside of your polygon.

27

Next let's take a look at how to stroke the edges of the octagon using a thick, red, rounded corners, stroke operation.

Stroking Shapes: Using Stroke to Edge Your Octagon in Red

To define the stroke color, also called stroke paint, as it is in Inkscape, click on the Stroke paint tab, and set a Red color by setting a Red slider to a value of 127 (this is 50%), and click the solid icon (second one), as shown in Figure 3-3.

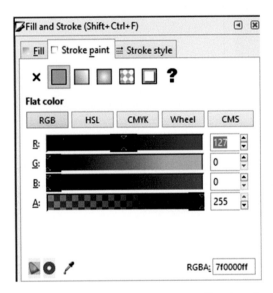

Figure 3-3. *Click Stroke paint tab in Fill and Stroke palette*

Since the default stroke width is one pixel, which would be nearly invisible to the naked eye, click on the Stroke style tab on the far right of the Fill and Stroke palette, as seen in Figure 3-4. Set the Stroke Width value to 20 pixels (px in your drop-down selector) and click the Round Join (middle) option to round the corners of your octagon. The Cap options are for open lines and curves, and you can play around with your Dashes and Markers settings, if you like, to style the line itself, which is always set to solid as a default as that is the most common usage.

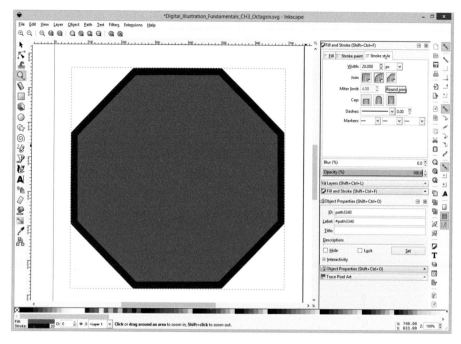

Figure 3-4. *Set a 20 Width, and Round Join, in Stroke style tab*

As you can see, at the bottom left, your stroke and fill attributes are summarized, as is the layer that you are drawing the shape on.

The **Opacity** of 100% is seen in gray at the bottom of the Stroke and Fill palette, on the right side of your screen. This will be applied to your stroke and fill settings. There's also a **Blur** slider you can play around with, which will apply a blur algorithm to your stroke and fill settings.

There is also an Opacity setting in your Layers palette, which we are going to cover in detail during Chapter 10. Next, let's take a look at how to use the Inkscape **Spiral** tool.

Spiral Shapes: Stroking Open Shapes Using Cap

Let's take a look at how to create an open shape so that we can take a look at that **Cap** feature in the Stroke style tab. Select the **Create spirals** tool, as shown in Figure 3-5, and use the default **Turns** setting of **3.00** and **Divergence** setting of **1.0,** and an **Inner radius** setting of **zero**. These tool options are set at the top left of Inkscape in the options toolbar. Next, click in the middle of the page, and pull out the spiral. You can not only control the size of this spiral, when you pull it out from the center, but also its rotation. Next, you can use the Fill and Stroke palette and its Stroke paint tab to set the stroke Flat color to an RGB color value of Blue 127, which is a 50% value between black and bright blue, giving you nice medium blue tones. The solid color icon and Flat color setting is seen highlighted in blue in Figure 3-5. In case you're wondering why 127 gives 50%, 127 is 128 (counting from zero), which is half of 256 values allowed for each 8-bit RGB color slider value range.

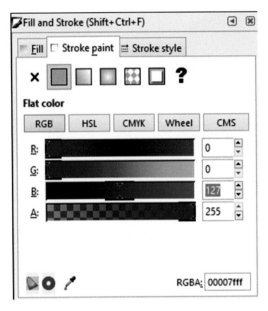

Figure 3-5. *Set Stroke paint to use an RGB Blue value of 127*

Next, click the Stroke style tab and set the **Width** value of **12** pixels, and select the **Straight Join** and **Round Cap** option icons, which are shown selected in blue in Figure 3-6.

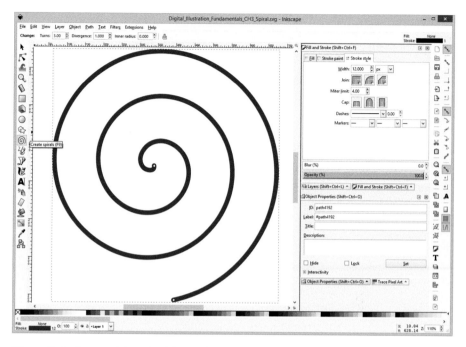

Figure 3-6. *Create a blue spiral, by stroking the spirals tool*

Try selecting some of the dashes option settings in your drop-down menu. With the Round Cap option, dashes look like hot dog (sausage) links tied together to create a spiral. You could experiment with all of these different settings for a lifetime!

As you can see at the bottom left, your stroke and fill attributes are summarized, as is the layer that you are drawing your shape on. Since this is an open shape, your Fill is set to None, and your Opacity is set to 100%. Let's take a look at how to use the Fonts installed in your workstation to create a Text object (shape) in Inkscape next, using the Create and Edit Text objects tool.

Font Shapes: Creating Text Shapes Using Fonts

Since using Fonts and Text is an important part of everyday multimedia production work, let's use an Inkscape text tool to create some gold Segoe Script text with a nice purple border for all of you Los Angeles Lakers fans out there. First, select Inkscape's Create and Edit Text objects tool, as seen in Figure 3-7, and set the Segoe Script font option at a size of 128, at the top left in the options toolbar. I left the other options as the default settings. Next, click in the middle of the page, and pull out the text. You can use the Fill and Stroke color palette, seen on the top right, to set the fill color to **Gold**, which is defined by setting **Red** to **127** and **Green** to **127** in **RGB**.

Figure 3-7. *Create a gold Segoe Script object using a text tool*

Next, click the Stroke style tab and set the **Width** value of **4** pixels, and select **Round Join** and **Round Cap** option icons, which are shown selected in blue in Figure 3-8. Since this is a script font, we want to use as many rounded edge settings as we can, since the font is rounded and flowing, not straight edged, like some other fonts are. For these fonts, the straight-edged stroke cap and join setting will of course be more appropriate.

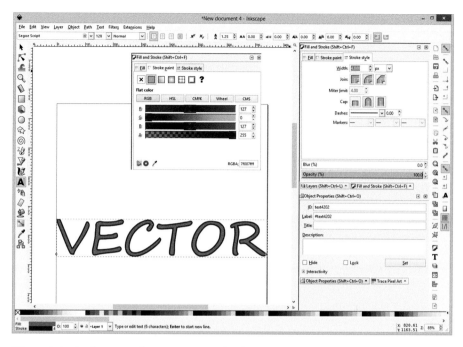

Figure 3-8. *Stroke a text object using 4 pixels of purple color*

Try selecting some of the dashes option settings in your drop-down menu to create text-based special effects. When you combine these different stroke settings with the different font libraries that are out there, you will find that there are many different visual effects you can attain for a client multimedia production project.

As you can see at the bottom left, your stroke and fill attributes are summarized, as is the layer that you are drawing the shape on, and the instructions for using the Text tool, the number of characters you have typed, and instructions regarding how to continue using the Text tool.

Summary

In this third chapter, we looked at how you can add color and style to your 2D vector illustration shapes using fill and stroke settings that invoke styling operations to be applied to the vector shapes by the 2D rendering engine. We looked at some new tools in Inkscape including the **polygon tool**, the **spiral tool**, and the **Text tool**. Since we have a lot to cover in this book, I wanted to cover the primary Inkscape tools that you are likely to use during this third chapter.

In the next chapter, you will take a look at a much more complex version of the fill, known as the **gradient**, and how to create these advanced fills in Inkscape.

CHAPTER 4

■ ■ ■

The Depth of Digital Illustration: Using Gradients

Now that we have covered the basic concepts regarding how to stroke and fill using solid color, we will get into the more complex 2D texturing algorithms available in SVG. These include color gradients, covered in this chapter, as well as seamless image patterns, which we will cover in Chapter 5.

In this chapter, we will look at the two different types of gradients supported in SVG and how to apply these to stroke and fill operations, which we just covered in Chapter 3. If you use the right colors in a gradient, it can make 2D look 3D.

Inkscape Illustration: Fill Gradients

Let's start out with Fill Gradients, as gradients are much more commonly used to fill your closed shape than they are to fill your (stroked) open shape. There are two different types of SVG gradients: radial gradients, which emanate from the center like a sunburst; and linear gradients where the colors stay parallel to each other. Both types of gradients can be very useful, and when they are used with the correct color "stop" settings, they can even simulate the look of a 3D object using 2D vector data.

Radial Fill Gradients: Enhancing Your Heart Shape

Let's use a radial fill gradient to add some more character to the heart object that you created in Chapter 2. Launch Inkscape and open your Digital_Illustration_Fundamentals_CH2.svg project file, and click on your **radial gradient icon** (the middle icon), which will place the current radial gradient inside your heart, as its current fill operation. As you can see in Figure 4-1, an **Edit gradient** icon will then appear at the bottom of the **Radial gradient** section of the dialog. We'll use this icon to edit the color (and transparency) gradient listed in the **Gradient table**.

© Wallace Jackson 2015
W. Jackson, *Digital Illustration Fundamentals*, DOI 10.1007/978-1-4842-1697-2_4

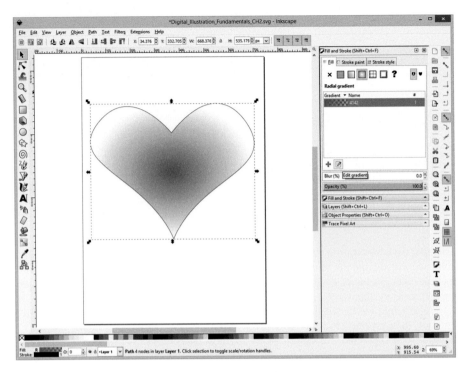

Figure 4-1. *Open CH2.svg; select Fill tab, Radial Gradient Icon*

The first thing we'll need to do is to edit the existing gold to a transparent gradient, to become more of a bright red to pink gradient. Click the **Edit gradient** icon and a gradient edit guide will appear over the top of your heart shape, as shown in Figure 4-2.

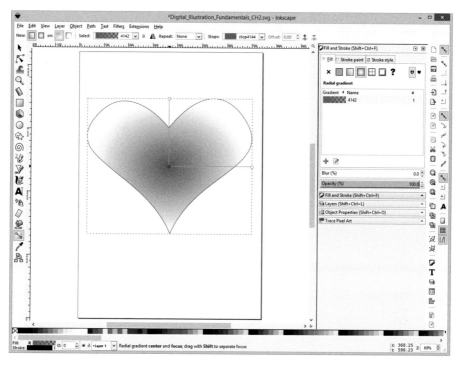

Figure 4-2. *In Edit Gradient Mode, select middle gradient stop*

The center node will allow you to position the center of the radial gradient, which I am going to position at the center of the heart. You can also offset the center of the gradient to achieve other special effects, for instance, simulating your 3D sphere. This can be simulated by using a radial gradient inside of a circle shape.

The ends of these handles, which emanate from the center node, can be used to control the **falloff** of the radial gradient effect. Play around with this gradient placement control handle interface, and become familiar with how it allows you to fine-tune your gradient placement within your shape fill operation.

Notice that when you click the Edit gradient icon that a Edit Gradient icon is also selected (activated) in the Inkscape toolbar at the left side of the user interface. At the top is a toolbar that contains 10 settings used for the gradient tool.

To change this first color "stop" in the gradient, click on the middle node in the gradient placement guide. This should select the stop4144 initial color in the gradient, which can be seen in the drop-down at the right of the gradient setting toolbar at the top of Inkscape, and place the color data in the tab on the right floating palette docking area so that you can edit it. This is shown in Figure 4-3 using the Flat color RGB slider controls, so that you can specify a **Bright Red** (**196**, or **77% Red** value) for the center part of your 2D vector heart object.

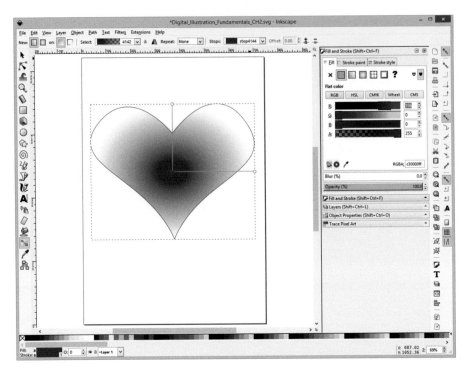

Figure 4-3. *Click Stroke paint tab in Fill and Stroke palette*

As you change the color from gold to red, you will see a change in real time, in your heart object in the canvas area of your Inkscape project. You will also see a **color swatch preview** in the **Stops** drop-down menu in the gradient settings toolbar at the top of Inkscape.

You will also see a **preview of the entire gradient** that you are creating in the **Select** drop-down menu, toward the left side of the gradient settings toolbar, at the top of Inkscape.

The next thing that you will need to do is to edit your other end of this gradient, so that it goes from the bright red to a pink or Teaberry heart color, on the outside of the heart.

To change the second color "stop" in the gradient, click one of the outer nodes in a gradient placement guide. This will select the **stop4146** initial color in the gradient, which can be seen in the drop-down at the right of the gradient setting toolbar at the top of Inkscape, and place the color data in the tab on the right floating palette docking area so that you can edit it. You could also select this stop from your **Stops** drop-down.

This can be seen in Figure 4-4, using the Flat color RGB slider controls, so that you can specify the **Teaberry Red** using **Red 180**, (a 70% Red value), **Green 60** and **Transparency 40** slider setting. The transparency setting equates to adding White color values, since your current background (paper) color is White.

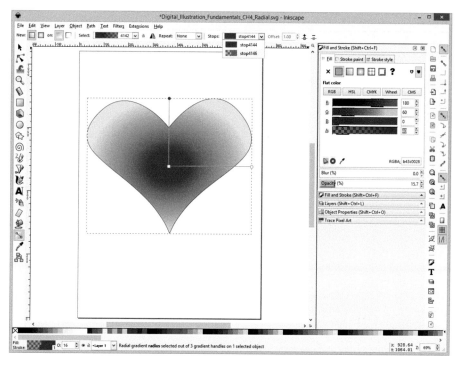

Figure 4-4. *Set a 20 Width, and Round Join, in Stroke style tab*

As you change the color from gold to red, you will see a change in real time, in your heart object in the canvas area of your Inkscape project. You will also see a color swatch preview in the Stops drop-down menu in the gradient settings toolbar at the top of Inkscape.

You will also see a preview of the entire gradient that you are creating in the Select drop-down menu, toward the left side of the gradient settings toolbar, at the top of Inkscape.

As you can see at the bottom left, your stroke and fill attributes are now updated with the new gradient settings, with the Layer 1 which you are drawing the shape on also specified.

Next let's take a look at how to use the Inkscape **Linear Fill Gradients** feature.

Linear Fill Gradients: Enhancing Your Text Object

Let's use a linear fill gradient and add some more character to the Text object that you created in Chapter 3. Launch Inkscape, and open your **Digital_Illustration_Fundamentals_CH3_Text_tool** project file, and click on the **linear gradient icon** (the third icon), which will place the current linear gradient inside your vector text object, as a current fill operation. As you can see in Figure 4-5, the **Edit gradient** icon should then appear at the bottom of the **Linear gradient** section of your dialog. We'll use this icon to edit the color (and transparency) gradient listed in the **Gradient table**, which Inkscape has generated, and named 4699. You can click next to this 4699 and give the gradient its own customized linear gradient name, if you feel like it.

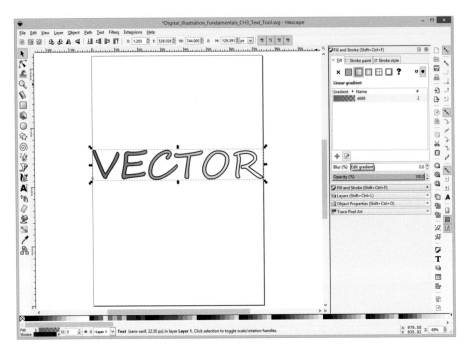

Figure 4-5. *Open CH3_Text project; select Fill, Linear Gradient*

The first thing that we will need to do is to change the direction of the linear gradient, which is currently defaulting to side-to-side. We want the gradient to run from top to bottom so that we can have a line of lit gold running through the text so that it looks more like metal.

To accomplish this, place your mouse over the round part of your gradient control handle until it turns red. Then, click and drag it, from the right side to the top of the bounding box around the text object, as is shown in Figure 4-6.

Figure 4-6. *Click Edit Gradient Icon, drag gradient end to top*

As you can see, in real time, this changes the direction of your gradient, making it a diagonal gradient, which you will now see is also a possibility.

To finish the operation, place the mouse over the square part of your gradient control handle, until it turns red. Then, click and drag it, from the left side to the bottom of the text object's bounding box, as shown in Figure 4-7.

41

Figure 4-7. *Insert a new linear gradient stop in the middle*

The next thing that we need to do is to add another stop so that we can have three color, and two color changes, in your gradient definition.

We want the outsides of your gradient (in this case, the top and bottom of the text object) to be gold and the inside to be yellow. So, the gradient will have three stops, the first of which will be gold, the second of which will be yellow, and the third will be gold again.

To add a stop, click on the **plus-node icon**, to the right of the Stops drop-down. I have highlighted it in blue in Figure 4-7 and left the tool-tip pop-up helper showing as well.

Click in the middle of the gradient line that is running vertically through your text object. This will insert a diamond using a red color, as is shown in Figure 4-7.

You can control the exact placement of this stop using a spinner labeled **Offset**, just to the left of your add and remove stop node icons, and just to the right of the Stops drop-down.

As you can see, in Figure 4-8, I have placed this middle stop exactly 50% of the way between the two existing stops, as is indicated by the 0.50 value in the spinner. Now all that you have to do is to reconfigure the three stop color values.

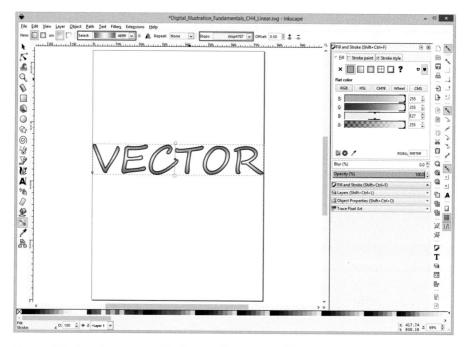

Figure 4-8. *Edit Stops to provide the metallic gradient effect*

Since your bottom (first) stop is set to gold already, click on the top (third) stop and set it to gold as well, by setting the Red and Green sliders to a color value of 127.

Next, click the middle stop; it will turn a blue color, and set the Red and Green sliders to 255, which is really 256, or 100% on, to give yourself a bright yellow color.

To blend the yellow color with the white background, and thus brighten it a bit more, set the Transparency to a value of 40, which equates to 16%.

As you can see in the **Select** or **Stops** drop-down swatches at the top of Inkscape, you are getting the "metallic cylinder" gradient effect, and a bright yellow color like sun glinting on gold in the middle, so that the linear gradient looks like gold tubing.

This bright reflection in both the radial and the linear gradient is called a **specular reflection** in 3D terminology, and is used to make 2D geometry look like it is 3D, using gradients of color. This is often called **2.5D** in the multimedia industry.

Next, let's take a look at using gradients inside stroke operations. Gradients can be just as useful in stroke operation applications, especially if you use a lot of open shape vectors in your 2D vector illustration artwork.

Inkscape Illustration: Stroke Gradients

Let's take a look at Stroke Gradients next, as gradients can also be used to **texture open shape paths**. The problem with the use of gradients with stroke operations is that the SVG command language does not support **conforming** the gradient to the path, so you can only apply the gradient across the entire open shape object. I will show you how to get around this limitation, and to achieve this effect by using **SVG filters**, which we will be dedicating an entire chapter to (Chapter 8) later on in the book. Let's apply a radial gradient to your spiral object that will make it fade from view around the perimeter of the spiral.

Radial Stroke Gradients: Enhancing Your Spiral

Open your **Digital_Illustration_Fundamentals_CH3_Spiral** project, and click the arrow (selection) tool at the top of the toolbar and select the spiral object. Next, click the Fill and Stroke palette and then the Stroke paint tab, and click on your **radial gradient icon**, which is the middle icon, as seen in Figure 4-9. Click the edit gradient icon, shown selected on the left in the toolbar, and position the center of the gradient at the source of your spiral, and the outer handles in the corners of the box (this is called a **bounding box**) containing your spiral object.

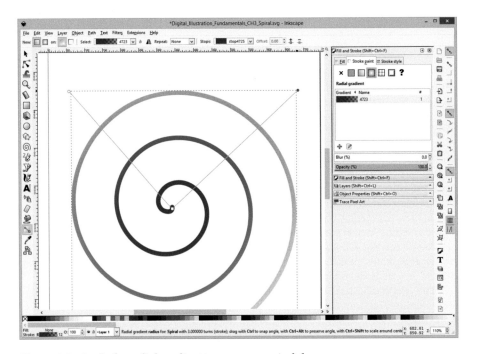

Figure 4-9. *Apply the radial gradient to your open spiral shape*

Click the **Edit gradient** icon at the bottom of the Radial gradient section of your dialog, and create a gradient with the first stop as Medium (50%) Blue and the second stop Transparent so that your spiral will slowly disappear. The gradient is seen at the top left of Figure 4-9.

If SVG could apply a gradient along a curve, I would have used a linear gradient that went from Dark Blue to Transparent (or white) to Dark Blue again, to create a 3D special effect on this spiral object. Unfortunately SVG does not support this yet so I'll have to show you another way to accomplish this special effect with **SVG filters**, which are supported in HTML5 and Java.

Use your **File ➤ Revert** to go back to your CH3_Spiral.svg project, or use **File ➤ Close**, and then **File ➤ Open**, and open it again, so that you have your solid Medium 50% Blue spiral back.

Drop-down the Inkscape **Filters** menu, and then select the **Bevels** menu, and then select the **Button** Bevel Filter, as can be seen at the top of Figure 4-10. Make sure your spiral object is selected, which you can see it is, in Figure 4-10, as indicated by the dotted line bounding box around your spiral object.

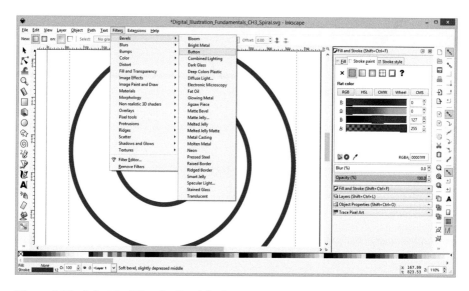

Figure 4-10. *Select the Filters ➤ Bevels ➤ Button menu sequence*

If you do not have an object selected, an SVG filter cannot apply its algorithm to anything, and it will abort with an error message. You can apply these same SVG filters in HTML5 in CSS3 code or JavaScript, and in Java using the JavaFX SVG APIs.

As you can see in Figure 4-11, this filter will give you the result that the linear gradient conforming itself to a path would give you, so, until the SVG command language will allow a gradient to "follow" the path, you can utilize this approach to get the special effects results that you are currently seeking.

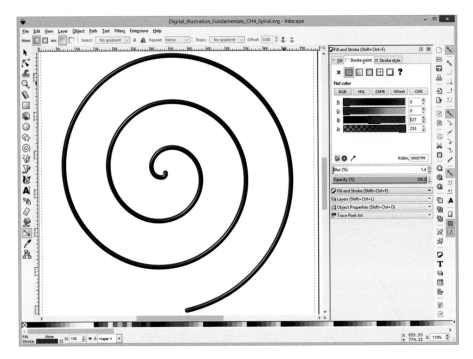

Figure 4-11. *The Button Bevel gives you in-path gradient effect*

One of the most powerful things about SVG is that it's a command-based programming language, which is why I am covering that aspect of it in detail in Chapter 7.

For this reason, your structures can be set up in such a way as to be able to accomplish many effects that you might not think were possible by using SVG in the form of an illustration software package, like Inkscape. This is especially true, given these SVG Filter capabilities, as you will see in Chapter 8.

Now that you have seen how powerful gradients and filter applications can be, you will need to take a look at how to use digital imagery in vector illustration using **seamless patterns**.

Summary

In this fourth chapter, we looked at how you can add color and style to your 2D vector illustration shapes using fill and stroke settings that invoke styling operations to be applied to the vector shapes by the 2D rendering engine. We looked at some styling effects that can be applied using radial gradients and linear gradients, as well as getting an introduction to SVG Filters to accomplish an effect that the gradients cannot currently provide to us. Since we have a lot to cover in this book, I wanted to cover the primary Inkscape **rendering effects** that you are likely to use during the fourth and fifth chapters.

In the next chapter, you will take a look at a much more complex version of texturing shapes using the **seamless pattern** and learn how to create these advanced patterns using GIMP 2.8.

■ ■ ■

CHAPTER 5

The Imagery of Digital Illustration: Using Patterns

Now that we have covered the basic concepts regarding how to stroke and fill using both solid colors and gradients, in this chapter we will cover the progressively more complex 2D imagery texturing **patterns** available in SVG. I will include the work process for creating seamless image patterns, which are much more effective and believable than patterns where you can see a seam (or more than one seam). Certain patterns, such as plaid or polka dots, are inherently tileable, if you set the tile up correctly.

In this chapter we'll look at how to create **bitmap image tiles** using GIMP 2.8, which can be used with Inkscape and SVG as patterns, and how to apply these to stroke and fill operations, which we covered during Chapter 3. This is the first area that SVG and vector illustration has addressed to span raster images and vector illustrations, as the 3D vector industry has done so successfully. There's a paid vector illustration package called **Corel Painter 2016** that turns digital illustration into digital painting by adding even more digital image features, and even a real-world physics engine, just like you'll find in 3D software packages such as Autodesk Maya, NewTek Lightwave, or Blender 3D.

Just in case you are thinking about taking your digital illustration to a higher level, I will be covering Painter 2016 in this book as well, as it is affordable given what if offers.

Inkscape Illustration: Using Fill Patterns

Let's use a fill pattern to add some more detail to the heart object that you created in Chapter 2. Launch Inkscape and open up your **Digital_Illustration_Fundamentals_CH2.svg** project file, and click on the **Fill** tab in the Fill and Stroke palette and then on the **Pattern icon** (the fifth icon), which will place the default Stripes pattern inside your heart as your current fill operation, as you can see in Figure 5-1. A Very Art Deco Heart!

© Wallace Jackson 2015
W. Jackson, *Digital Illustration Fundamentals*, DOI 10.1007/978-1-4842-1697-2_5

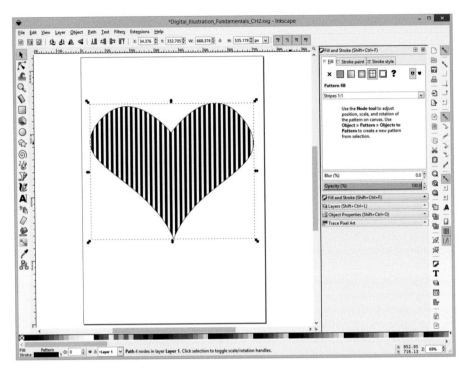

Figure 5-1. *Open CH2.svg and select the Fill tab's Pattern Icon*

The Stripes algorithm shown in Figure 5-1 is actually an SVG command syntax algorithm or program of sorts that uses the vector command language to create the pattern effect seen here.

If you drop-down this **Pattern fill** menu, there are a ton of vector patterns already defined for you. If you want to look ahead in the chapter, Figure 5-9 shows a portion of this menu.

You might be wondering, Hey could I use my own patterns, and can they be bitmap images that are tiled together to fill, or stroke, my vector illustrations? The answer is yes, and that is what the chapter is all about: how exactly to bridge digital imaging and digital illustration together, to allow artisans to generate greater visual impact for their digital illustrations.

In fact, I'll cover this topic more and more as the book progresses, as after I have covered the fundamentals of SVG, I am going to cover digital painting, with Painter 2016, as well. I cover Painter 2016 in detail in my *Digital Painting Techniques* title (Apress, 2015).

The first thing that we will need to learn is how to use GIMP 2.8.14 to create a bitmap pattern to use in Inkscape. Your bitmap creations can use the same four bitmap file formats that are currently supported for HTML5, Java, JavaFX, and in Android Studio 1.4. These formats include JPEG, BMP, GIF, and PNG.

Using GIMP: Creating Your Image Pattern

If you have not downloaded and installed the open source GIMP 2.8.14 digital image editing and compositing software yet, go to `http://www.gimp.org` and click an orange **Download** button, and then install this software package on your digital illustration workstation. After it's installed launch it! Let's get to work!

Click your **background color swatch**, shown circled on the right side of Figure 5-2. You can tell by an icon that white is your background color currently, because it appears as if it is **behind** the black (foreground) color icon. This is numbered with a one in Figure 5-2, and shows a **Change Background Color** picker dialog below it. I set a Red Hue value of **zero**, **48%** saturation, and **96%** lightness value, which equates to RGB values of **Red 245** (96% Red), **Green 127** (50% Green), and **Blue 127** (50% Blue). These values will give you a nice "Teaberry" heart background color.

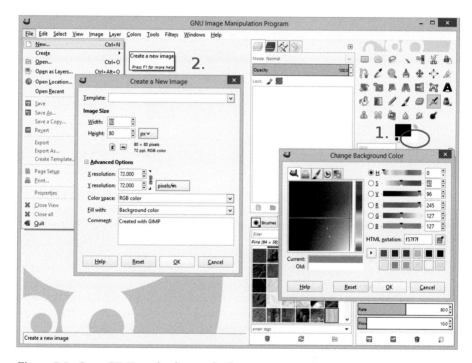

Figure 5-2. *Open GIMP; set background color; create a new image*

Step two, seen on the left side of Figure 5-2, is to use a **File ➤ New** menu sequence and open the GIMP **Create a New Image** dialog. Set an **80 pixel** Width and Height using a **72 DPI** X and Y resolution, and specify the **RGB Color Space**.

Set **Fill with** to **Background color**. This is why you set up your Teaberry background color as step one in the work process.

As you can see in Figure 5-3, your Background layer now has an appropriate background color for your heart object, and you can select a circular area using a circle and ellipse tool. This tool is shown selected in blue at the top right of Figure 5-3 in the **tool icons palette** of GIMP. In the **Tool Options** tab under the tool icons, I selected **Antialiasing**, and **Expand from center** as tool options, and drew out a circular selection area. I also clicked the **foreground color swatch** and set that to **Red**.

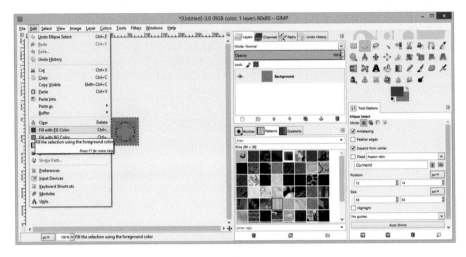

Figure 5-3. *Select circular area; use Edit ➤ Fill with FG Color*

The circular selection area is shown on the left side of your screen, as is the **Edit ➤ Fill with FG Color** menu sequence, which is what you should use to tell GIMP to fill the selection you just created with a Red color for your Heart object pattern fill, which you are creating here using digital image software.

If you want the Red circle on a **different layer** than the background color, just to provide you with a little taste of my GIMP 2.8.14 knowledge outlined in the *Digital Image Compositing Fundamentals* (Apress, 2015) title I wrote previous to this one, click on the Background layer to select it and then right-click and select a **New Layer** context-sensitive menu option. This will instruct GIMP to create a new layer to hold your Red Circle.

Be sure that you create this new layer **before** you invoke your **Edit ➤ Fill** menu sequence, so that you are directing GIMP to place your Red Fill Color on the new layer instead of over the background fill color on the Background layer.

Whichever work process (one layer or two layers) you use is fine to achieve the same result, so pick one, implement it, and then utilize the **Select ➤ None** menu sequence to remove the selection, now that you have used it to create your Red Circle. This menu sequence can be seen in Figure 5-4 on the left side.

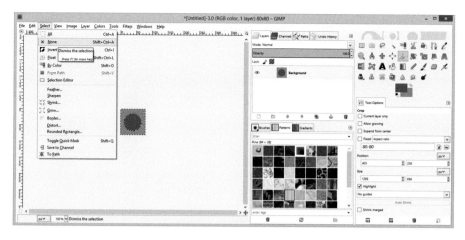

Figure 5-4. *Deselect circle, using Select ➤ None menu sequence*

As you can see in the **Layers** tab in the middle I decided to use my Background layer to hold my pattern composition. Next use the **File ➤ Export As** menu sequence, shown in Figure 5-5, to export (save) this pattern by using a bitmap image file format.

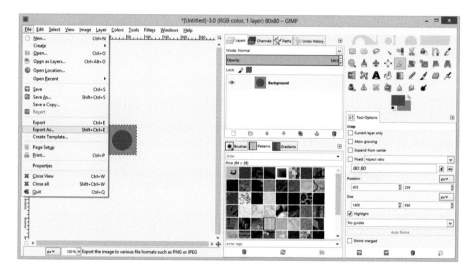

Figure 5-5. *Use File ➤ Export As to save a pattern as a bitmap*

In the Export Image dialog, type the **PolkaHeart.png** file name in the Name field at the top of the dialog, as is shown in Figure 5-6, selected in blue. This file extension for your file name, that is, the .PNG part of the file name, will inform GIMP which bitmap file format (encoding algorithm) that you want the image data to use. I prefer a lossless .PNG (pronounced "Ping") image data format, as it provides the best visual results.

51

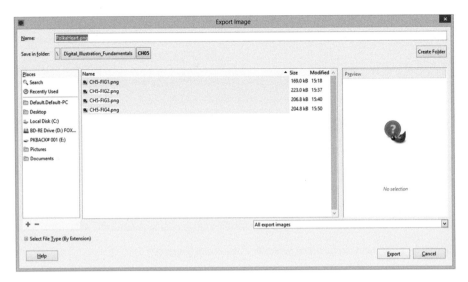

Figure 5-6. *Name the image file PolkaHeart.png and click Export*

Click on the **Export** button to export your bitmap pattern to the directory on your hard disk drive that you selected with the **Places** pane of the Export Image dialog on the far left. The folder hierarchy I used was E:\Digital_Illustration_Fundamentals\CH05.

The next thing that we need to do is to show you how you can install these custom bitmap image patterns inside Inkscape.

Imagery in Illustration: Bitmap Patterns

Now that I've shown you how to utilize the popular open source GIMP digital image compositing software to create a tileable bitmap image pattern for use inside of Inkscape, it is time to show you the work process for installing your own custom bitmap image artwork. This will allow you to **bridge** your digital image compositing pipeline with your digital illustration content creation pipeline. Inkscape will do this as an SVG command file generator with pattern functions; more advanced 2D illustration software, such as Corel Painter, take the concept even farther.

Using Bitmap Images as Fill: Inkscape Pattern Fill

Let's use a bitmap-based fill pattern this time to add far more visual interest to the heart object that you created in Chapter 2. Open Inkscape, using your Digital_Illustration_ Fundamentals_CH2.svg project file, by double-clicking on the file in your file manager, or right-click the file, and use Open with Inkscape. Use the **File ➤ Import** menu sequence, as shown in Figure 5-7, to open the **Select file to import** dialog. Navigate to and select a **PolkaHeart.png** file, and then click the **Open** button, which will then open the **png bitmap image import** dialog seen at the bottom of Figure 5-7.

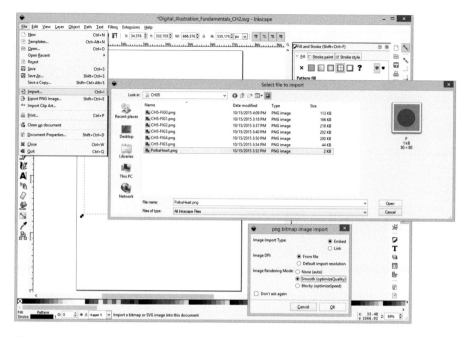

Figure 5-7. *Use File* ➤ *Import; select Embed and Smooth options*

Select the **Embed Image Import Type**, and select the **Image DPI From file** radio button option as well. I suggest using your **Smooth (optimizeQuality)** setting for your **Image Rendering Mode**, and I leave **don't ask again** unchecked, so I can always specify my preference for the SVG command language syntax that Inkscape is going to generate.

Once all of these settings have been specified, click on the **OK** button and you should see your bitmap pattern tile asset in the middle of Inkscape; in this case, it would be on the top of your Heart object, as is shown in the middle of Figure 5-8.

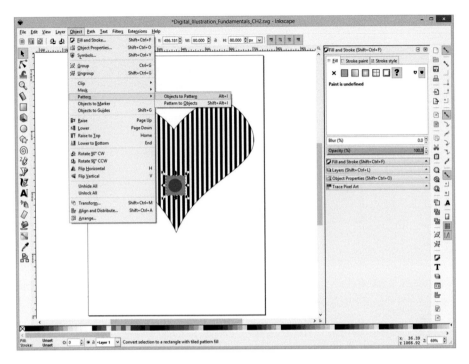

Figure 5-8. *Use Object ➤ Pattern ➤ Objects to Pattern function*

The next step in the work process, also shown at the top of Figure 5-8, is to use Inkscape's **Object ➤ Pattern ➤ Objects to Pattern** menu sequence, to invoke the Inkscape function, which converts bitmap objects into patterns that can be used in fill and stroke operations.

Next, click the **arrow icon** at the top left of Inkscape's toolbar, and move your bitmap pattern object, out of the way of your composition and off of the page.

As you can see in Figure 5-8 and later, I placed mine at the lower right-hand corner of the Inkscape document.

Click on your heart object to select it for editing. In the Inkscape Stroke and Fill palette, select your **Fill** tab, and then select the Pattern icon, as shown, fifth from the left, in Figure 5-9.

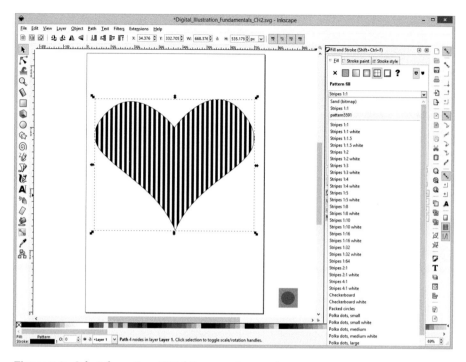

Figure 5-9. *Select the pattern5591 bitmap pattern option to set*

In the **Pattern fill** section of the dialog, use the drop-down menu to select your **pattern5591** option, which is what the SVG command syntax generator named the pattern in the previous Objects to Pattern function.

The pattern appears in your top (recently used patterns) part of your drop-down selector, because you recently added it.

As you can see in Figure 5-10 the heart now looks great!

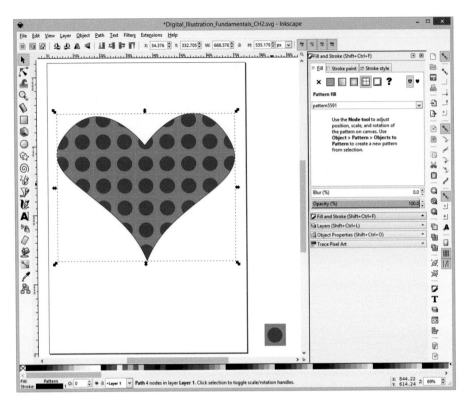

Figure 5-10. *The bitmap image pattern will fill the heart shape*

Next, let's take a look at how you will use this pattern to apply a stroking operation to this heart shape. I will use a different fill pattern for the interior of your heart shape, to make the bitmap pattern stroke stand out more clearly.

Using Bitmap Image Strokes: Inkscape Pattern Fill

As you can see in Figure 5-11, I have selected a different fill pattern from the drop-down, called Cloth (bitmap). This is so that you will be able to visualize the differentiation between the fill and the stroke bitmap imagery.

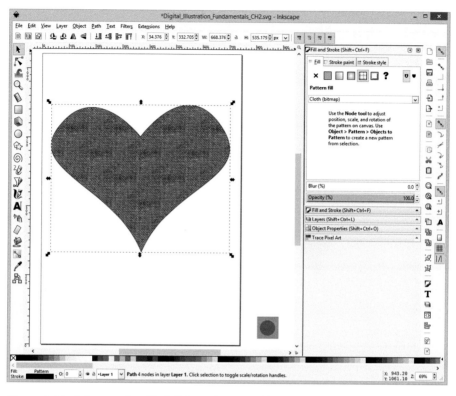

Figure 5-11. *Select another Cloth (bitmap) pattern fill option*

Next, click on the Stroke style tab and set the Width to a setting of 72 pixels, using your square **Cap** and **Join** settings afforded by the icons shown on the top right of Figure 5-12.

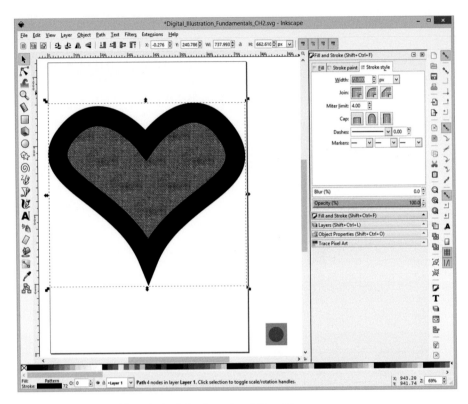

Figure 5-12. *Set a wider, 72 pixel, Stroke style width setting*

This will create a thick black border, around your heart object, which is what we will be filling with the custom bitmap pattern that you created in GIMP earlier in the chapter.

Next, click on your Stroke paint tab, and set your drop-down to pattern5591, as is shown at the top right of Figure 5-13.

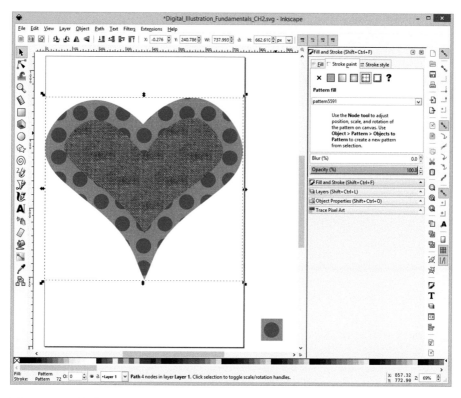

Figure 5-13. *Set bitmap pattern5591 as the Stroke paint pattern*

This will create the pattern stroke for your thick black border around your heart object using the custom bitmap pattern that you had created in GIMP earlier in the chapter.

Next, we will take a closer look at the different vector 2D digital illustration file formats.

Summary

In this fifth chapter, we looked at how you can use patterns to add digital imagery to the strokes and fills for your 2D vector illustration shapes. We looked at the work process for using the GIMP digital image compositing software package to create tiles to use as bitmap patterns, as well as at the work process for importing and applying these inside of Inkscape.

In the next chapter, you will take a look at an Inkscape work process for **rendering SVG into different file data format** containers so that you can transfer your work among different platforms and software packages.

CHAPTER 6

■ ■ ■

The Rendering of Digital Illustration: Data Formats

Now that we have covered the basic concepts regarding how to create vector shapes as well as stroking and filling them using solid colors, gradients, and patterns, in this chapter we show how you export the SVG command data created and generated by Inkscape 0.91 into other popular raster (PNG), vector (EPS), publishing (PDF), application programming (JavaFX), and similar file formats.

Since we looked at the File ➤ Import work process in the previous chapter, in this chapter we will look at **File ➤ Export** and **File ➤ Save As** work processes and learn how to "render" SVG data, which is what an Inkscape composition really is, in other popular content formats.

After we have taken a look at this, we will look at your actual SVG command language syntax in Chapter 7 on SVG Command Language and how it works at a fundamental level.

Inkscape PNG Export: Rendering Objects

Let's take a look at how to "render" or "rasterize" that heart object that you have been refining over the course of the book. Rendering is a popular concept these days, in both 2D and 3D as well as i2D and i3D new media content genres. Since both 2D and 3D vector assets are essentially draw commands, data points and styling (texturing) information, the rendering (or rasterizing) process turns these into RGB pixel data and alpha channels, so that they can be used in a digital imaging context, with image codecs (image formats) and in image compositing pipelines.

Launch Inkscape with `Digital_Illustration_Fundamentals_CH5.svg`, which is the project file from the previous chapter, and select the bitmap tile object at the bottom right of Inkscape with the arrow tool, and hit your **Delete** key. Then use the **File ➤ Export PNG Image** menu sequence, shown in Figure 6-1, on the top left.

© Wallace Jackson 2015
W. Jackson, *Digital Illustration Fundamentals*, DOI 10.1007/978-1-4842-1697-2_6

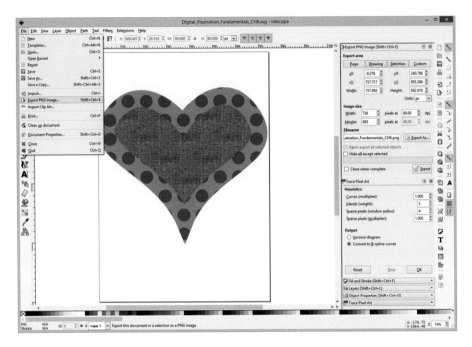

Figure 6-1. *Open CH5.svg and select File* ➤ *Export PNG Image*

If you want to open a project that already has the image tile deleted, you can open
`Digital_Illustration_Fundamentals_CH6.svg`.

It is important to note that once you have installed the bitmap tile pattern into
Inkscape, you could delete that object within your project file; just don't delete the image
file that Inkscape is referencing from your hard disk drive. Do not move this file's location,
as that would change its path reference.

Invoking this File ➤ Export PNG Image menu sequence will add an **Export PNG
Image** palette to the very top of the Inkscape palette docking area. This is located on the
right side of your user interface, and it is shown on the top right of Figure 6-1.

Since you don't have anything selected yet, your buttons at the top of this Export
PNG Image palette are set ambiguously until you select the entire page (**Page**), an entire
illustration (**Drawing**), or an SVG object within the composition (**Selection**).

Once you select your heart object using the **arrow select** tool, the **Selection** button
at the top of this palette should be auto-selected by Inkscape, and you can set all the other
options to suit what you need in a digital image compositing pipeline.

I checked the **Hide all except selected**, which I'm hoping will create an alpha
channel (object transparency mask) for me, as well as the **Close (palette) when
complete** checkbox (option).

After all the settings are ready for export, click on the **Export As** button, seen in blue on
the right in Figure 6-2. This will bring up the **Select a filename for exporting** dialog, shown
in Figure 6-3. Name your file **PolkaHeartStroke.png** and click on the **Save** button to save it
in the directory you have specified at the top of the dialog using the file management utilities.
I used my `E:\Digital_Illustration_Fundamentals` folder to save the file.

62

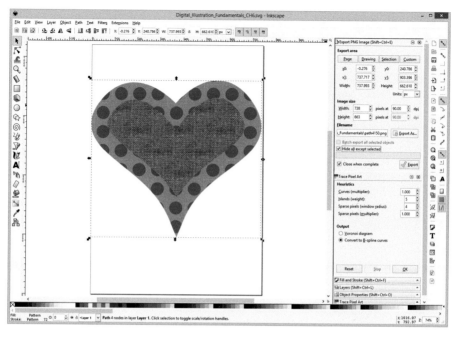

Figure 6-2. *Select the heart object and set the export settings*

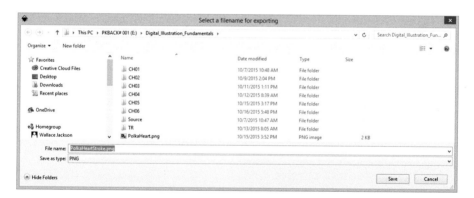

Figure 6-3. *Name the PNG heart image asset PolkaHeartStroke.PNG*

Now you have specified where you want to store the file. Click the **Export** button, shown in Figure 6-4 on the right. This instructs Inkscape to render your SVG data into this PNG file.

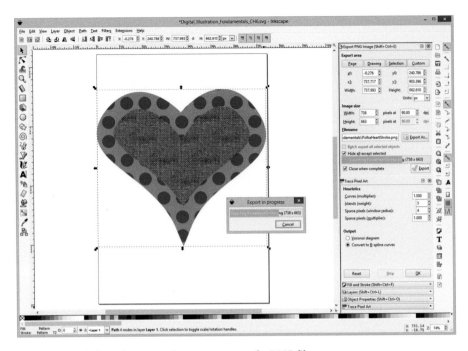

Figure 6-4. *Click on the Export button to export the PNG file*

The next thing that we're going to do is to use the GIMP digital image editing package to see if Inkscape has created an alpha channel for us. If it has, we will see a transparent area around our heart object. GIMP represents transparency using the checkerboard pattern, as you can see on the left in Figure 6-5.

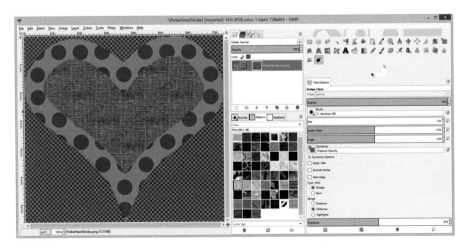

Figure 6-5. *Use GIMP to open the PNG file to preview the result*

Inkscape will also export using other popular vector and publishing formats using the **File ➤ Save As** menu sequence. This is technically not rasterizing the data, but it could be called rendering the data in another format, either pixels (raster) or otherwise, as you will see in the next section of this chapter.

Inkscape Vector Export: Using Save As

All the other formats that Inkscape supports exporting SVG data in are accessed using the **File ➤ Save**, **File ➤ Save As** or **File ➤ Save As Copy** menu sequences. I use Save As if I have a project, or Save As Copy if I need to save a copy. The Save As menu sequence will open the Select file to save to dialog, as seen in Figure 6-6, with the format selector drop-down menu open.

Figure 6-6. *The Select file to save to dialog and its options*

As you can see on the extensive drop-down menu, Inkscape supports dozens of multimedia production industry file formats, including Adobe Acrobat or Flash (but not Illustrator, a direct competitor to Inkscape), Postscript, Java (using JavaFX), HTML5, and many more. We cannot cover all 27 in this chapter, but I'll cover the most popular open source formats (Java, PDF, and EPS), as these are the ones you're most likely to use to either print or publish content with. Encapsulated Postscript can be used to print, or as an alternate to the AI (Adobe Illustrator) format, which is not supported in Inkscape, as it is a patented format, which is proprietary to Adobe Illustrator. Let's take a look at Adobe Acrobat Reader's rich document publishing platform first.

Exporting to Adobe Acrobat Reader: PDF Format

Let's select the Adobe Acrobat Portable Document Format (*.pdf) option first, as shown selected in blue in the drop-down menu selector in Figure 6-6. This will open the **Select file to save to** dialog shown in Figure 6-7. Once you click the **Save** button, you will get the **Portable Document Format** dialog shown on the right side of Figure 6-7 (I combined two screenshots into one) where you can set your PDF document format file export options, before clicking on the **OK** button, to export your SVG as a PDF.

Figure 6-7. *Use File ➤ Import; select Embed and Smooth options*

You can use a Restrict to PDF version drop-down menu to select a PDF version to utilize, and select options to **Convert texts to paths**, **Omit text in PDF, and create a LaTex file**; and to **Rasterize filter effects**, which we'll be covering in Chapter 9 covering SVG Filters, which can apply special effects for SVG illustration content production pipelines, making art look like it was created using digital image compositing software.

I named my PDF file `Digital_Illustration_Fundamentals.pdf` and then opened it up in Adobe Acrobat Reader to preview the result of the Inkscape PDF export algorithm, as shown in Figure 6-8.

Figure 6-8. *Use Object ➤ Pattern ➤ Objects to Pattern function*

Next, let's take a look at the EPS vector image format. This can be used in your digital illustration software package, such as Adobe Illustrator, as well as in your digital imaging software packages like Corel Painter 2016 or Adobe Photoshop, and in 3D software packages such as Blender or Autodesk 3DS Max 2016. The EPS format can also be used with Postscript printers.

Exporting to Encapsulated Postscript: EPS Format

Let's select the Encapsulated Postscript Format (*.eps) option next, as shown eighth on the list shown in the drop-down menu selector seen in Figure 6-6. This will open the **Select file to save to** dialog shown in Figure 6-7. Once you click the **Save** button, you will get the **Encapsulated Postscript** dialog seen on the right side of Figure 6-9 (I again combined two screenshots into one to save space) where you can set your Postscript Level and other format file export options similar to the PDF export options, before clicking on the **OK** button, to export your SVG illustration as an EPS file. If you send the file to your laser printer or open it in Illustrator, you will see your 2D heart.

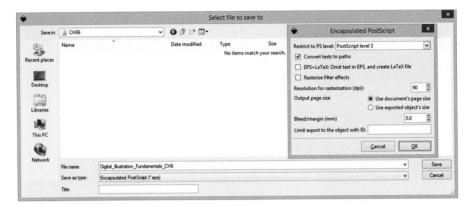

Figure 6-9. *Select the pattern5591 bitmap pattern option to set*

Next, let's take a look at how you can export Java code, so that you can have Inkscape code Java in Digital Illustration Fundamentals Java Classes for you, based on your SVG commands!

Exporting to JavaFX: Publish in Java and Android

Let's select the JavaFX data format (*.fx) option next, which is shown as number 12 on the drop-down menu that is shown in the Save as type format selector in Figure 6-6. This will open the **Select file to save to** dialog for JavaFX, which can be seen in Figure 6-10. Whatever you name your JavaFX programming code export in this dialog will also be the class name for your Java class that Inkscape is about to write Java code for once you click on the **Save** button (it should be a **Code** button!).

Figure 6-10. *The bitmap image pattern will fill the heart shape*

Once you click the **Save** button, Inkscape will generate a Java Class for your 2D heart, which I opened in Notepad, and is shown in Figure 6-11 with some code formatting (indenting).

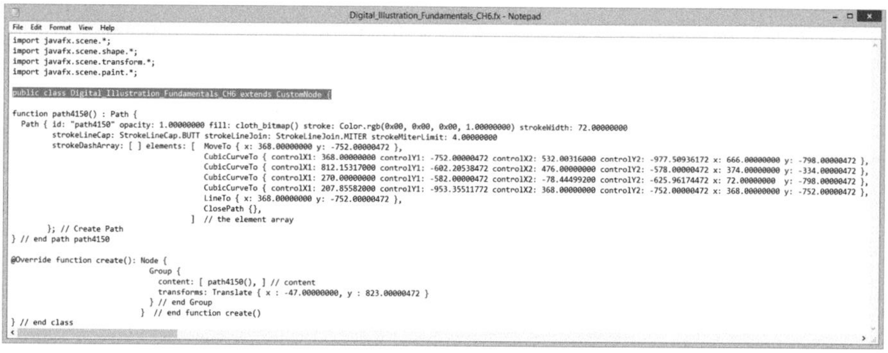


```
import javafx.scene.*;
import javafx.scene.shape.*;
import javafx.scene.transform.*;
import javafx.scene.paint.*;

public class Digital_Illustration_Fundamentals_CH6 extends CustomNode {

function path4150() : Path {
  Path { id: "path4150" opacity: 1.00000000 fill: cloth_bitmap() stroke: Color.rgb(0x00, 0x00, 0x00, 1.00000000) strokeWidth: 72.00000000
         strokeLineCap: StrokeLineCap.BUTT strokeLineJoin: StrokeLineJoin.MITER strokeMiterLimit: 4.00000000
         strokeDashArray: [ ] elements: [  MoveTo { x: 368.00000000 y: -752.00000472 },
                                           CubicCurveTo { controlX1: 368.00000000 controlY1: -752.00000472 controlX2: 532.00316000 controlY2: -977.50936172 x: 666.00000000 y: -798.00000472 },
                                           CubicCurveTo { controlX1: 812.15317000 controlY1: -602.20538472 controlX2: 476.00000000 controlY2: -578.00000472 x: 374.00000000 y: -334.00000472 },
                                           CubicCurveTo { controlX1: 270.00000000 controlY1: -582.00000472 controlX2: -78.44499200 controlY2: -625.96174472 x: 72.00000000  y: -798.00000472 },
                                           CubicCurveTo { controlX1: 207.85582000 controlY1: -953.35511772 controlX2: 368.00000000 controlY2: -752.00000472 x: 368.00000000 y: -752.00000472 },
                                           LineTo { x: 368.00000000 y: -752.00000472 },
                                           ClosePath {},
                                        ]  // the element array
        }; // Create Path
} // end path path4150

@Override function create(): Node {
                              Group {
                                content: [ path4150(), ] // content
                                transforms: Translate { x : -47.00000000, y : 823.00000472 }
                              } // end Group
                            }  // end function create()
} // end class
```

Figure 6-11. *Showing the Java class code generated by Inkscape*

The Inkscape package should get you 99% of the way there as far as Java coding goes, but you will still need to clean up the Java and JavaFX code a bit, for you Java coders out there.

Still, this is a pretty impressive feat for illustration software: writing a Java class using the JavaFX SVG APIs. We'll be looking at the SVG command data, shown in the middle of your Java code in Figure 6-11 in Chapter 7, which covers SVG Command Syntax, and how to get Inkscape to generate it for you.

Summary

In this sixth chapter, we looked at how you can use Inkscape's Export and Save As features to render or convert your 2D vector illustration shapes into other new media file formats or content publishing formats. We looked at the work process for exporting your heart object into a number of formats popular worldwide, including the PNG32 digital image (raster) format; the EPS digital illustration (vector) format; the PDF rich media document publishing format; and the Java 7, 8, and 9 (JavaFX) code format utilized in Android Studio, iOS, or Java application publishing.

In the next chapter, you will take a look at an Inkscape work process for **editing SVG command syntax** so you can transfer your work among different platforms and software packages, as well as further customizing your SVG illustrations using a text editing software tool such as Notepad, NetBeans, or IntelliJ.

■ ■ ■

CHAPTER 7

The Syntax of Digital Illustration: SVG Commands

By now you have an understanding of how to export to some of the major new media content publishing formats by using the export and save as functions in Inkscape. So it's time to get a bit more advanced and look inside the **SVG command syntax** that is inside many of these formats. The SVG markup language is based on XML and is a lot like HTML as well, using tags and parameters. Many of you will be familiar with how a markup language functions.

We'll look at the primary SVG commands first, and then we will examine some examples of how path data and style parameter settings are specified, using **SVG XML**. You will examine several of your Inkscape projects, after you export them to SVG command syntax, using the **Plain SVG** XML-based file format.

SVG Syntax: Coding Vector Shape Data

There are 10 different letters that can be utilized with your numeric path (X,Y data point coordinate location) data in SVG data strings. Each of these SVG command letters has an uppercase (absolute reference) and lowercase (relative reference) version. You can combine all of these scalable vector graphics SVG commands with Java and JavaFX classes to create interactive vector (digital illustration) artwork that has never before been experienced. In fact, I have already showed you this in Chapter 6, where you got a preview of how SVG syntax looks. You will see a lot more SVG command syntax in this chapter, wrapped in XML markup, rather than Java classes.

SVG Command Summary: Lines, Arcs, and Curves

SVG data commands provide you with a great deal of flexibility to define shape paths made of lines and curves for your digital illustration content applications, as you can see in Table 7-1.

© Wallace Jackson 2015
W. Jackson, *Digital Illustration Fundamentals*, DOI 10.1007/978-1-4842-1697-2_7

Table 7-1. *Primary SVG commands to utilize for creating SVG path data*

SVG Command	Symbol	Type	Parameter	Description
moveto	M	Absolute	X, Y	Defines a Start Of Path at the X,Y using absolute coordinates
moveto	m	Relative	X, Y	Defines a Start Of Path at the X,Y using relative coordinates
closepath	Z	Absolute	None	Close SVG Path, by drawing line from last to first point
closepath	z	Relative	None	Close SVG Path, by drawing line from last to first point
lineto	L	Absolute	X, Y	Draws a Line from the current point to the next point
lineto	l	Relative	X, Y	Draws a Line from the current point to the next point
horizontal lineto	H	Absolute	X	Draws Horizontal Line from current point to next point
horizontal lineto	h	Relative	X	Draws Horizontal Line from current point to next point
vertical lineto	V	Absolute	Y	Draws a Vertical Line from current point to next point
vertical lineto	v	Relative	Y	Draws a Vertical Line from current point to next point
curveto	C	Absolute	X,Y, X,Y, X,Y	Draws a cubic Bézier curve from current point to next point
curveto	c	Relative	X,Y, X,Y, X,Y	Draws a cubic Bézier curve from current point to next point
Short and smooth curve	S	Absolute	X,Y, X,Y	Draws a cubic Bézier curve from current point to next point
Short and smooth curve	s	Relative	X,Y, X,Y	Draws a cubic Bézier curve from current point to next point
quadratic Bézier curve	Q	Absolute	X,Y, X,Y	Draws a quadratic Bézier curve (current point to next point)
quadratic Bézier curve	q	Relative	X,Y, X,Y	Draws a quadratic Bézier curve (current point to next point)
short quadratic Bézier	T	Absolute	X,Y	Draws a short quadratic Bézier (current point to next point)

(continued)

Table 7-1. (*continued*)

SVG Command	Symbol	Type	Parameter	Description
short quadratic Bézier	t	Relative	X,Y	Draws a short quadratic Bézier (current point to next point)
elliptical arc	A	Absolute	rX, rY, Rot	Draws an elliptical arc from current point to next
elliptical arc	a	Relative	rX, rY, Rot	Draws an elliptical arc from current point to next

An optimal way to see how to use these powerful SVG data path drawing commands is to get down to learning a work process for creating SVG data with vector illustration tools and export workflows. You will learn how to do this using Inkscape, using the "quick and dirty" approach, that is, let Inkscape do 99% of the path creation work. Then if you like, you can cut and paste these command data strings into your Java or JavaScript logic.

If you're a game programmer, you can also use these path data constructs as **collision detection polygons** and for similar **non-graphical uses** of vector data relating to **boundaries** rather than visual 2D rendered digital illustration artwork. If you're interested, I cover a workflow to do this using JavaFX's **SVGPath** class in *Beginning Java 8 Games Development* (2015) from Apress.

SVG Fills: Filling Your Closed Shapes with Color

As you have seen already, once you have defined your shape using lines, arcs, and curves, you can fill it to make it solid rather than hollow or empty. A fill can be a color, a gradient, or a tiling image pattern. You can fill an open shape if you like, and the (imaginary) line connecting the start point with the end point will define the fill boundary, so the fill does not go all over the place in your digital illustration! The fill operations, as well as the stroke operations, which we have also covered, are what are known as "painting" operations.

SVG Solid Color Fill: Filling Your Shape with a Solid Color Value

To fill the green octagon you created earlier in Chapter 3, a fill="green" command statement should be added, after your path data statement. This creates a shape that would be filled with a green color. Using SVG XML, these two declarations would be inside of a path XML tag, using the following SVG XML markup data structure to create a plain green octagon using only code:

```
<path>
d = "M 60 0 L 120 0 L 180 60 L 180 120 L 120 180 L 60 180 L 0 120 L 0 60"
fill = "green"
</path>
```

Solid fill color is not as useful as gradients, however, as careful use of gradients can even simulate a 3D result using 2D SVG graphics. Defining a gradient is more complex, so let's take a look at a linear and radial gradient SVG command syntax.

Gradient Fills: Linear Gradients and Radial Gradients

Much of what applies to how a linear gradient is set up in SVG command syntax will also apply to the radial gradient as well, which simply uses a different XML tag. I'll show you how to set up the <linearGradient> tag using SVG in XML, and you can simply change it later to be a <radialGradient> to change your gradient type. Gradients are defined using <defs> (definitions) tag in SVG XML. The <defs> tag goes inside the "parent" <svg> parent tags, which have the <linearGradient> tag as "children" tags. Inside this <linearGradient> tag are at least two <stop> child tags. As you know, Stops are used to define the colors in your gradient, what percentage the color takes up in an overall gradient, or an alpha or transparency value for that section of the gradient. There must be at least two stops, and you can use any amount of gradient sections that you need as well, via XML.

Make sure that your stop offset values add up to 100% in the end. Here is how you would fill your octagon with a red and yellow linear gradient; as you can see, it's much more complex:

```
<svg xmlns='http://www.w3.org/2000/svg' height="300" width="300">
  <defs>
    <linearGradient id="LinearGradient" x1="0%" y1="0%" x2="100%" y2="0%">
      <stop offset="0%" style="stop-color:rgb(255,255,0);stop-opacity:1" />
      <stop offset="100%" style="stop-color:rgb(255,0,0);stop-opacity:1" />
    </linearGradient>
  </defs>
  <path>
    d="M 60 0 L 120 0 L 180 60 L 180 120 L 120 180 L 60 180 L 0 120 L 0 60"
    fill="url(#LinearGradient)"
  </path>
</svg>
```

You wire the gradient into your fill using the id="name" parameter inside of the <linearGradient> tag and then reference that name inside of your fill="url(#name)" parameter, inside of the <path> tag, as you can see in the above XML markup example.

SVG Pattern Fills: Filling Your Shape with a Tilable Image Pattern

Patterns are also defined in the <defs> or "definitions" tag in SVG XML. The <pattern> tag goes inside the parent <defs> tag, and has the <image> tag as a child tag. Inside the <image> tag is a reference to, and specifications for, the image asset. As you know, patterns are seamless image tiles that fill shapes with a 2D texturing effect and are also usable with strokes.

Make sure your pattern width and height values match up with your image width and height values. The image X and Y are positioning the start of the pattern at the upper-left corner, which is always location 0,0. Here is how you would fill your octagon with an eight pixel tiling image pattern; as you will see, it's an even more complex definition than your gradient:

```
<svg xmlns='http://www.w3.org/2000/svg' height="300" width="300">
  <defs>
      <pattern id="pName" patternUnits="userSpaceOnUse"
              width="80" height="80">
          <image xlink:href="data:image/PolkaHeart.png"
                  x="0" y="0" width="80" height="80">
          </image>
      </pattern>
  </defs>
  <path>
    d="M 60 0 L 120 0 L 180 60 L 180 120 L 120 180 L 60 180 L 0 120 L 0 60"
    fill="url(#pName)"
  </path>
</svg>
```

I am showing you how to code this in case any of you are Android Studio developers, HTML, JavaScript, or Java application developers. Most digital illustrators can use software packages such as Inkscape or Illustrator to create vector artwork, later exporting it to the Plain SVG XML format to generate this code. I will be showing you this work process in the next section of this chapter, using the vector illustrations we have created so far during the book (the Heart, Octagon, and Filtered Spiral).

At the end of the workday, however, you'll need to know how to bridge these SVG commands with the multimedia publishing code, so I am going to cover the basic SVG commands during this chapter, so that you have knowledge regarding SVG and XML work processes for Android, JavaFX, and HTML application development.

The Stroke: Controlling How Lines and Curves Look

Finally, let's take a look at how to stroke, or color, style, or thicken, the lines, arcs, or curves that you created using these SVG commands. The stroke parameters will allow you to define stroke color, opacity, a width in pixels, dash array pattern, and how lines will be capped or joined together, using round, square, or bevel constants. Let's add all of these stroke-related parameters to the <path> that I created earlier for the octagon, and give it a 3 pixel thick black border, with rounded corners, a dashed line, and a 50% opacity, using the following SVG XML markup command syntax structure:

```
<path>
d = "M 60 0 L 120 0 L 180 60 L 180 120 L 120 180 L 60 180 L 0 120 L 0 60"
fill = "green"
stroke = "black" stroke-width = "3" stroke-dasharray = "5, 10, 5"
stroke-linecap = "square" stroke-linejoin = "round" stroke-opacity = "0.5"
</path>
```

Next let's finish up by looking at the SVG data commands that would be generated by the Inkscape projects you've created thus far, during the first six chapters of this book.

Inkscape Projects: SVG Command Syntax

Since vector new media assets are inherently optimized, as long as you use the smallest number of vertices (points and their data coordinates) possible to create your 2D (and 3D) assets, and the correct types of Bézier splines (curve types) for your objective, we will focus during this chapter more on how to use Inkscape to create these 2D vector assets and how to use Export functions to turn these into command data and XML markup that you can utilize not only in Android Studio, but also in JavaFX, JavaScript, and in HTML5, primarily by properly using XML and CSS. I'll cover some minor data footprint optimization pointers at the end of the chapter regarding replacing highly accurate float numerics with nearly as accurate (short) integer numbers.

Polygons: SVG Commands for Basic Closed Shape

Polygon shapes, which we covered in Chapter 3 on styles, are shapes that have straight lines on their perimeter, like triangles, squares, pentagons, hexagons, or octagons. These are created with path data using basic **MoveTo** and **LineTo** commands. Let's open the CH3_Octagon SVG file we created using Inkscape's polygon tool and turn this into SVG command syntax data. Use a **File ➤ Save As** menu sequence, shown in Figure 7-1, and save the file as **Plain SVG** XML, so we can take a look at SVG XML syntax.

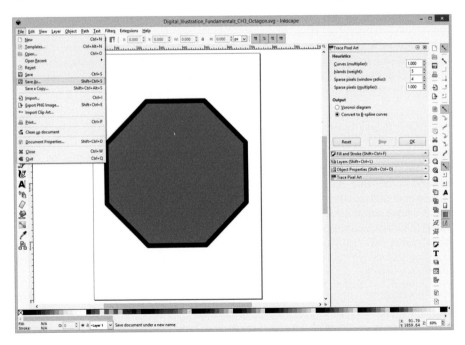

***Figure 7-1.** Open CH3_Octagon.svg and use File ➤ Save As feature*

Next let's look at the File ➤ Save As Plain SVG feature.

SVG Polygon Data Export: Using the File ➤ Save As ➤ Plain SVG

Inkscape uses File ➤ Save As to save different data formats, as you learned in the previous chapter. Save your Octagon as Plain SVG, as seen in Figure 7-2, appending "_Commands" to your name.

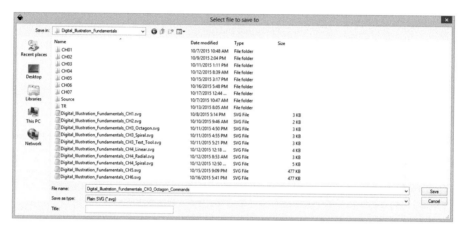

Figure 7-2. *Use File ➤ Save As menu sequence; select Plain SVG*

Once you have given your **Plain SVG** file its custom name, such as `Digital_Illustration_Fundamentals_CH3_Octagon_Commands.svg`, you will be able to differentiate it from the Inkscape artwork SVG.

Next, find the file on your hard disk drive and open the SVG XML data using a plain text editor. On Windows 8 this would be Notepad. You can right-click on the file name and select the **Open with Notepad** option to accomplish this quickly and easily.

Polygon SVG Syntax Editing: SVG XML Tags and Commands

The next step in the work process is to open the Plain SVG XML file in your text editor, as shown in Figure 7-3. I like to use Notepad for Windows. The **path data** string is shown in blue, and this is your raw SVG command syntax data for drawing your path for your object; in this case it is an Octagon. Notice that it uses the SVG letter commands from Table 7-1. The path object itself is defined using the SVG XML <path> tag, and **d=** (data) parameter. Inside the <path> tag there's also an **id=** and **style=** parameter option as well, for specifying a path name, assigned by Inkscape in this instance, and your style option settings.

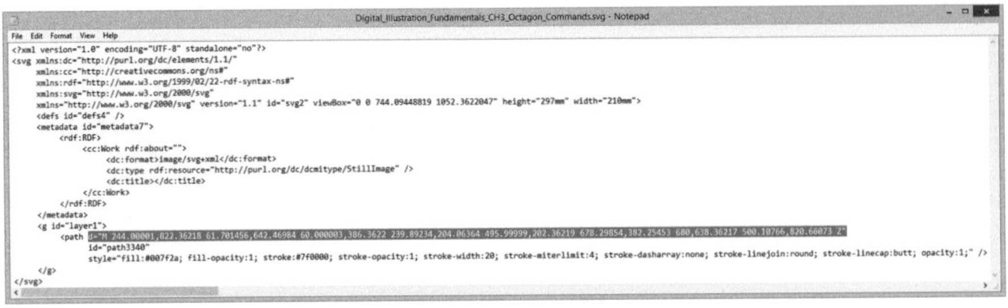

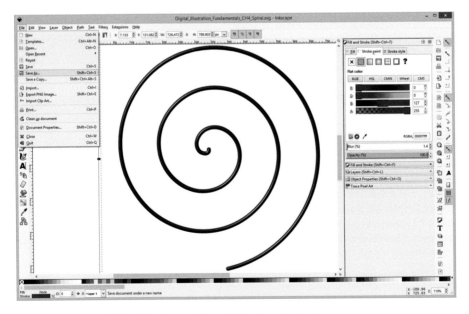

Figure 7-3. *Open CH3_Octagon_Command.svg file in a text editor*

Later on in this chapter, we will take a look at how to optimize this <path> d= data, as well as data inside other SVG XML tags.

Spirals: SVG Commands for Basic Open Shapes

Spiral shapes, which we covered during Chapter 4 on strokes and fills, are open shapes that have lines or curves that are not connected (closed), spirals, arrows, asterisks, crosses, or helixes. These are created with path data using basic **MoveTo, CurveTo,** and **LineTo** commands. Let's open the **CH4_Spiral.SVG** file we created using Inkscape's spiral tool and turn this into SVG command syntax data. Use a **File ➤ Save As** menu sequence, shown in Figure 7-4, and save the file as **Plain SVG** XML, so we can take a look at SVG XML syntax.

Figure 7-4. *Open CH4_Spiral.svg and use File ➤ Save As feature*

Use the Select file to save to dialog to save the spiral in the Plain SVG file format, as seen in Figure 7-5. Notice I'm again appending "_Commands" to a filename, keeping the original SVG file that contains the project artwork intact. If you name both files the same name, the OS will replace your Inkscape SVG with the Plain SVG that you are using to contain your SVG code.

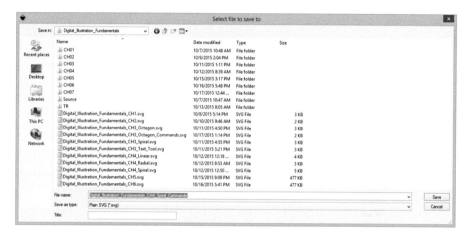

Figure 7-5. *Use File ➤ Save As menu sequence; select Plain SVG*

Open this **CH4_Spiral_Command** Plain SVG XML file in your text editor as shown in Figure 7-6. As you can see, the **filter effect** (abbreviated as "fe" in XML markup) makes this SVG data definition significantly more complex. This time I show a style filter parameter reference in blue at the bottom, and how it is connected to the <filter> tag, at the top, inside of the <defs> tag. Notice that your shape object path's data string is always contained inside of the <g> tag, which stands for "group."

Figure 7-6. *Open the CH4_Spiral_Command.svg file in text editor*

Notice this object uses the a start point (MoveTo) and a Bézier Curve (CurveTo) and creates the entire spiral structure by using only two SVG Commands (letter m and c) from Table 7-1, with the rest being curve vertex coordinates. This means you'll be able to data optimize this data string significantly, using the integer approach I will show you at the end of the chapter. Since this is a fundamentals book, I won't get into the complex XML **<feFilterName>** tags creating this filter effects structure.

Gradients: SVG Commands for Your Heart Shape

Custom shapes, such as the Bézier Heart we created in Chapter 2 and then styled in Chapter 4 covering stroke and fill are more complex shapes featuring closed curves, gradients, or patterns. These are created with path data using **MoveTo, CurveTo** and **LineTo** commands. Let's open the **CH4_Radial.SVG** file we created using the Inkscape Bézier Path tool and convert to SVG command syntax data. Use your **File ➤ Save As** menu sequence, as shown in Figure 7-7, and save the file as **Plain SVG** XML, so you can take a look at SVG XML syntax.

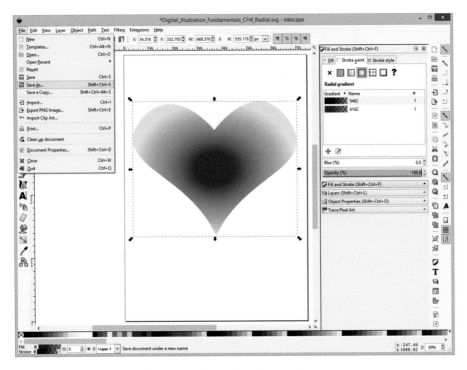

Figure 7-7. *Open CH4_Radial.svg and use File ➤ Save As feature*

Use a Select file to save to dialog to save the heart in Plain SVG format, appending "_Commands," as seen in Figure 7-8.

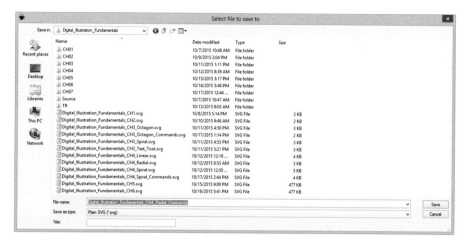

Figure 7-8. *Use File ➤ Save As menu sequence; select Plain SVG*

Open this **CH4_Radial_Command** Plain SVG XML file in your text editor as shown in Figure 7-9. As you can see, the **Linear Gradient** and Radial Gradient structures are again defined using the <defs> tag before they are used in the <g> tag's <path> tag using the style parameter's fill:url and stroke:url definitions, which reference the id= parameters defined for these gradients.

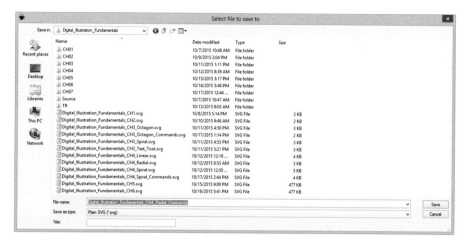

Figure 7-9. *Open the CH4_Radial_Command.svg file in text editor*

Make sure to closely examine how these gradient and stop tags relate to each other in the markup. Notice in the Inkscape file, seen in Figure 7-7, that I have replaced the black stroke around the heart object with a black to transparent, and red to transparent, radial gradient stroke to give it a more subtle or natural look and to generate a more complex SVG XML markup for you to examine and learn about SVG Commands, and SVG XML, from.

SVG Data Optimization: Integer Values

Let's take a look at the SVG command data in Figure 7-9 more closely to see if it can be optimized. As you'll see, the coordinate data uses extreme precision floating-point accuracy. This is seldom necessary for applications that write to screen display devices, although it may be necessary for printing to a billboard or on the side of an office building. For this reason a wise optimization work process is to round the floating-point values to become integer values. These data values will use far less system memory in Android Studio applications, a JavaScript application, or a JavaFX application, as integers are allocated far less memory space than a floating point, often 100% to 200% less memory space, depending on how Java logic defines numbers.

As you can see in Figure 7-10, the amount of data for a heart object is significantly less than what is shown in Figure 7-9. For many digital illustration projects this reduction will be even more significant, as you will see after I optimize your spiral object, shown in Figures 7-4 through 7-6, next.

Figure 7-10. *Convert your floating-point data into integer data*

It is important to note that if you have complex, multilayered projects, there's also a **Layers as Separate SVG** option, which is shown in Chapter 6 at the bottom of Figure 6-6, so you can keep your SVG Path command data modularized layer by layer. This is especially useful if you are coding JavaFX, for iOS and Android, or coding for Android Studio 1.4, using Java 7and XML.

Let's take a look at the SVG command data in Figure 7-6, so we can see if it can be optimized. Open your Spiral_Command SVG file, if it is not still open on your desktop, so that you can optimize the SVG command data string values inside of your <path> tag, d= parameter's string data values. As you see, the coordinate data uses extreme precision floating-point accuracy.

If you compare Figure 7-6 with Figure 7-11, you will see that the reduction in SVG command data, which is inside the d= parameter, in the area inside the quotation marks, can be quite significant, in this case 60% to 70% less data, or 100% to 200% less memory overhead as we're using 16-bit integer memory areas instead of 32-bit or 64-bit floating-point memory locations.

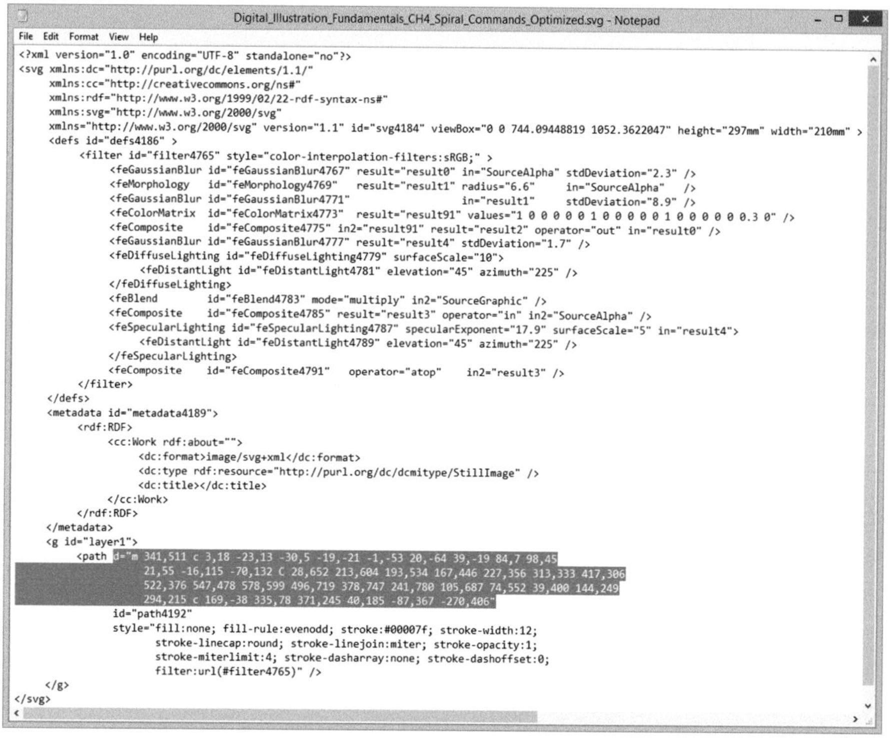


```
<?xml version="1.0" encoding="UTF-8" standalone="no"?>
<svg xmlns:dc="http://purl.org/dc/elements/1.1/"
     xmlns:cc="http://creativecommons.org/ns#"
     xmlns:rdf="http://www.w3.org/1999/02/22-rdf-syntax-ns#"
     xmlns:svg="http://www.w3.org/2000/svg"
     xmlns="http://www.w3.org/2000/svg" version="1.1" id="svg4184" viewBox="0 0 744.09448819 1052.3622047" height="297mm" width="210mm" >
     <defs id="defs4186" >
          <filter id="filter4765" style="color-interpolation-filters:sRGB;" >
               <feGaussianBlur id="feGaussianBlur4767" result="result0" in="SourceAlpha" stdDeviation="2.3" />
               <feMorphology   id="feMorphology4769"   result="result1" radius="6.6"     in="SourceAlpha"   />
               <feGaussianBlur id="feGaussianBlur4771"                  in="result1"     stdDeviation="8.9" />
               <feColorMatrix  id="feColorMatrix4773"  result="result91" values="1 0 0 0 0 0 1 0 0 0 0 0 1 0 0 0 0 0 0.3 0" />
               <feComposite    id="feComposite4775" in2="result91" result="result2" operator="out" in="result0" />
               <feGaussianBlur id="feGaussianBlur4777" result="result4" stdDeviation="1.7" />
               <feDiffuseLighting id="feDiffuseLighting4779" surfaceScale="10">
                    <feDistantLight id="feDistantLight4781" elevation="45" azimuth="225" />
               </feDiffuseLighting>
               <feBlend        id="feBlend4783" mode="multiply" in2="SourceGraphic" />
               <feComposite    id="feComposite4785" result="result3" operator="in" in2="SourceAlpha" />
               <feSpecularLighting id="feSpecularLighting4787" specularExponent="17.9" surfaceScale="5" in="result4">
                    <feDistantLight id="feDistantLight4789" elevation="45" azimuth="225" />
               </feSpecularLighting>
               <feComposite    id="feComposite4791"   operator="atop"    in2="result3" />
          </filter>
     </defs>
     <metadata id="metadata4189">
          <rdf:RDF>
               <cc:Work rdf:about="">
                    <dc:format>image/svg+xml</dc:format>
                    <dc:type rdf:resource="http://purl.org/dc/dcmitype/StillImage" />
                    <dc:title></dc:title>
               </cc:Work>
          </rdf:RDF>
     </metadata>
     <g id="layer1">
          <path d="m 341,511 c 3,18 -23,13 -30,5 -19,-21 -1,-53 20,-64 39,-19 84,7 98,45
                    21,55 -16,115 -70,132 C 28,652 213,604 193,534 167,446 227,356 313,333 417,306
                    522,376 547,478 578,599 496,719 378,747 241,780 105,687 74,552 39,400 144,249
                    294,215 c 169,-38 335,78 371,245 40,185 -87,367 -270,406"
               id="path4192"
               style="fill:none; fill-rule:evenodd; stroke:#00007f; stroke-width:12;
                    stroke-linecap:round; stroke-linejoin:miter; stroke-opacity:1;
                    stroke-miterlimit:4; stroke-dasharray:none; stroke-dashoffset:0;
                    filter:url(#filter4765)" />
     </g>
</svg>
```

Figure 7-11. *Optimized path data values for your spiral object*

The SVG command values inside of this d= data string are what will go inside of an Array object in your Java, JavaFX, or JavaScript code, so this is the primary area in SVG that you'll want to optimize from a game programming, content publishing or application development standpoint.

I felt it was important to show this bridge between your digital illustration workflow and your applications development and publishing (and possibly programming) workflow, because the publisher of this book (Apress) specializes in programming and technical or scientific educational books. Hope you don't mind!

Summary

In this seventh chapter, we looked at **SVG Command Syntax** and how the **SVG XML** standard is used to **export** digital illustrations as data, which can later be modified and utilized in other content publishing platforms, and in open source programming languages. This is important if you ever wish to **bridge** your illustrations into the world of interactive application development, by using popular open source content development platforms such as Java, JavaFX, JavaScript, HTML5, Kindle, iOS, Blackberry, and Android.

In the next chapter we take a look at how to "vectorize" raster imagery, using the Inkscape Trace tool and work process.

CHAPTER 8

■ ■ ■

The Vectorization of Digital Imagery: Image Tracing

Now that you have a solid understanding of how to export Plain SVG XML data for your programming and content publishing work process, let's take a look at one of the Inkscape tools that will employ a complex vectorization algorithm to do all of the work for you. You have already learned that your vector artwork can be "rendered" into a raster, pixel, or bitmap format, and in this chapter you will learn how to go in the other direction.

We'll look at the Inkscape **Trace Bitmap** algorithm, which will take the input bitmap image that you import into Inkscape, just like you did in Chapter 5, and "vectorize" it with complex algorithms that analyze the pixels in the image and create your 2D vector illustration SVG data, using your pixel pattern data.

Inkscape Trace Bitmap: Vectorize Images

Inkscape has a very impressive tool that is accessible using a Path ➤ Trace Bitmap menu sequence and that implements a complex algorithm, actually a series of algorithms with a front-end UI in a multi-tabbed control panel configuration, which we will be taking a look at over the course of this chapter. Inkscape uses the **Potrace** bitmap tracing engine by **Peter Selinger**. If you want to find out more about this software or get a stand-alone version, visit the http://potrace.sourceforge.net code repository. Inkscape has plans to support other vectorization algorithms in the future. Since this Potrace bitmap tracing engine is now the vectorization tool currently in place in Inkscape we will focus on this during this chapter, as it does a great job turning the bitmap images that you import into Inkscape 0.91 into 2D vector illustration artwork for you and does this automatically. This can save you a ton of time tracing over images manually using the Bézier Path tool, so I think you'll like this chapter quite a bit. Let's get started because algorithms can be a lot of fun to play around with and utilize, as they do your work for you!

© Wallace Jackson 2015
W. Jackson, *Digital Illustration Fundamentals*, DOI 10.1007/978-1-4842-1697-2_8

Digital Image Source: Using Inkscape File ➤ Import

The first thing we need to do is to find a bitmap image with a cool object in it that would look good as a vector shape object to trace. There is a 3D car rendering that I use in my digital image compositing and Android programming titles that fits this bill nicely, so we will use that. It is shown in Figure 8-1 and is named: **Digital_Illustration_Fundamentals_CH8_3D_Car.png**.

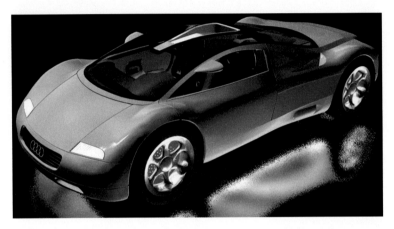

Figure 8-1. *A 640KB CH8_3D_Car.png bitmap at 964 by 512 pixels*

Open Inkscape, and use a **File ➤ Import** menu sequence, as seen in Figure 8-2, to import the CH8_3D_Car.png digital image.

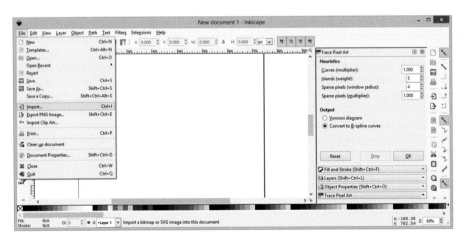

Figure 8-2. *Use File ➤ Import menu sequence; open CH8_3D_Car.png bitmap image*

This will bring up the **Select file to import** dialog seen on the left side of Figure 8-3. Since I haven't created my book repository files yet, I used the CH8-FIG1.png file, instead. As you can see, this dialog shows you that your file is 964 by 512 pixels. Click your **Open** button, which brings up your **png bitmap image import** dialog, and select the **Embed Image Import Type** and set **None** for your **Image Rendering Mode**. Get your **Image DPI** from this digital image file that you are importing. Once you've set up all of these image import options, click on your **OK** button.

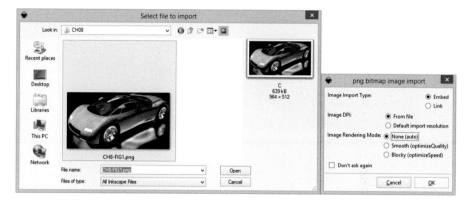

Figure 8-3. *Import 3D Car image using Embed type and Image DPI From file*

After your digital image appears in Inkscape, select the arrow tool, and then select and move your image into the center of Inkscape, so that you can see it better.

Trace Bitmap Algorithm: Configuring Parameters

Now you are ready to apply the digital image tracing algorithm to this PNG24 image. This algorithm will analyze the pixel data in the image based on color and contrast, and then devise how to apply vector elements (lines and curves) to it using the settings that you configure in the **Trace Bitmap** dialog, which is the primary subject of this section of the chapter. Use the Inkscape **Path ➤ Trace Bitmap** menu sequence, shown at the top of Figure 8-4, and open the Trace Bitmap dialog, so that we can take a look at the different panels that are organized using tabs, much like the floating palette docking area on the right side of Inkscape.

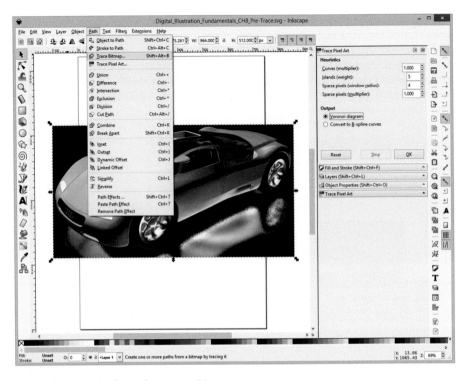

Figure 8-4. *Invoke the Path ➤ Trace Bitmap menu sequence*

There are three tabs in the Trace Bitmap dialog, as seen in Figure 8-5. The first is the **Mode** tab, shown in the far-left panel in Figure 8-5, which allows you to set an operational, or functional, mode for this Trace Bitmap algorithm. The second is the **Options** tab, shown in the middle panel in Figure 8-5, which has options for suppressing speckles, which are isolated pixels as those of you who use Photoshop know from using the despeckle filter, as well as smoothing corners and optimizing path data.

Figure 8-5. *Review the options in all three of the dialog tabs*

There is also a **Credits** tab, shown on the far-right side of Figure 8-5, which has the Potrace web site and programmer name in it. Click on the **Live Preview** check box, as I did in that tab to turn on the preview of what all of these tab settings should do once you activate them.

Let's start with the bottom part of your Mode tab, as is shown in Figure 8-6. Select the Colors option, and you will see that your Preview on the right is now showing the vectorization in color. This is shown on the left side, in Figure 8-6. If you select your Grays radio button option, you will see the similar result, only in grayscale, using no colors (in this case, red). If you select one of these three radio buttons, you'll generate multiple scans that create a group of path objects in your SVG XML output. Other selections, at the top, will generate one big contiguous path data object.

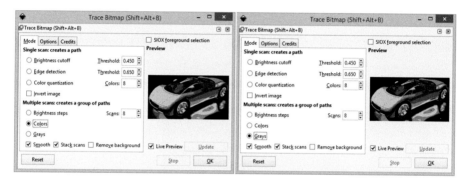

Figure 8-6. *Preview the Colors and Grays Multiple scans options*

Next let's take a look at the **Single scan creates a path** section at the top of the Mode tab, as shown in Figure 8-7. The **Brightness cutoff** option, shown on the left side of Figure 8-7, uses the **grayscale value** of a pixel as an indicator for whether it should be considered to be black or white. The **Threshold** can be set from **zero**, which is **black** (or, off), up to **one**, which is **white** (fully turned on), similar to how an alpha channel works.

Figure 8-7. *Preview the options under the Single scan section*

The **Edge detection** radio button selector will produce an intermediate bitmap that will look the least like your original image. This mode is similar to the Brightness Threshold, except it only detects edges, and therefore, it will provide lines and curves that would otherwise not be produced by the algorithm.

This is the setting I am going to use to trace this car. The **Threshold** setting for Edge detection adjusts the brightness threshold to control whether any pixel that is adjacent to the contrasting edge will be included in the trace. The setting can therefore adjust the darkness (or thickness) of any edge in the output. The edge detection algorithm was devised by J. Canny as a way of finding any iso-clines that are of similar contrast.

The **Color quantization** radio button filter will find the edges where the image color changes, even at uniform brightness and similar contrast levels. A **Number of Colors** setting decides how many output colors there would be if a bitmap was in color. It then decides black or white value based on whether the color has an even or an odd index value.

Next, let's move the source bitmap image up so that when we generate the trace, we get a combination of these two (color image plus trace output), as shown in Figure 8-8. You are doing this so that you have room to move the image portion aside and then see the resulting curves that this tracing tool generates.

Figure 8-8. *Drag the source image object to the top of Inkscape*

Select the Edge detection radio button option, and click on the **OK** button, to apply the Bitmap Trace Algorithm.

As you can see in Figure 8-9, a path overlays the image.

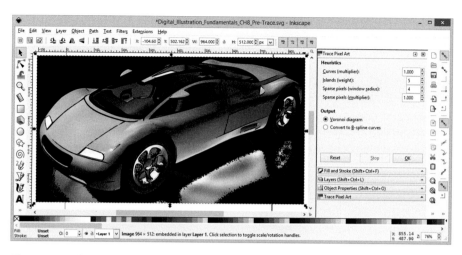

Figure 8-9. *The trace output initially overlays a source image*

You'll have to pull the source image down and out of the way of the trace using the arrow tool, as shown in Figure 8-10.

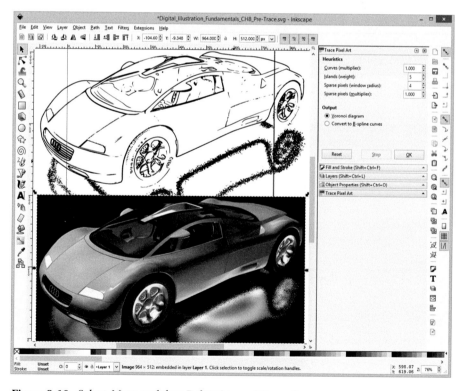

Figure 8-10. *Select, Move and then Delete Source Bitmap Imagery*

Once you have pulled your source bitmap from behind your trace data, hit your delete key, and delete it so that you can save just the vector data, just like we did in Chapter 7, so we can take a look at the SVG XML and the SVG Command string data.

Optimizing Your Illustration: Export Plain SVG Data

I saved just the trace data in an Inkscape SVG format using the name **Digital_Illustration_Fundamentals_CH8_Trace.svg** and then a **Digital_Illustration_Fundamentals_CH8_Trace_Command.svg** file to analyze using an OS text editing tool.

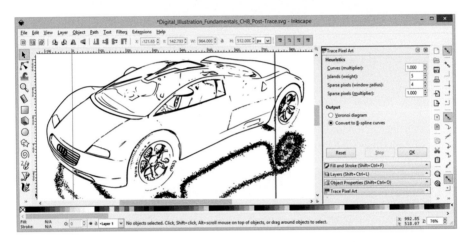

Figure 8-11. *Save a Plain SVG file named CH8_Trace_Commands.svg*

As you can see, in Figure 8-12, your SVG data is held in one massive path object. The <path> tag is highlighted in blue.

Figure 8-12. *Review an CH8_Trace_Commands.svg file SVG+XML data*

Since Notepad can't handle all of the vector data that a trace algorithm generates, another great way to get a view of a data footprint is using the file management utility. In Windows this is called Explorer. As you can see, the source image's SVG file is 866KB, both image and a trace is 1271KB, and your trace alone is 407KB. 407 plus 866 is 1273, as shown in Figure 8-13.

Figure 8-13. *Use file manager to see raster and vector filesize*

Next, let's apply the **Multiple Path; Colors** Bitmap Trace algorithm setting. As you can see in Figure 8-14, you'll get an entirely different result, featuring eight sets of <path> data.

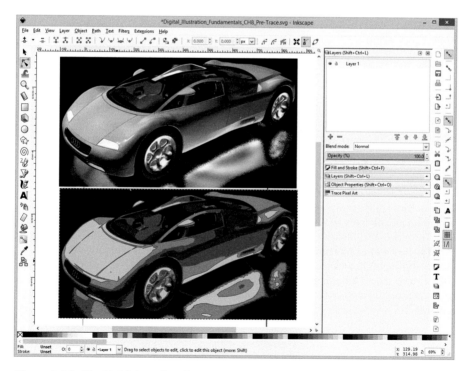

Figure 8-14. *The Multiple Path Colors option creates many paths*

93

As you can see, in Figure 8-15, your SVG data is held in multiple <path> objects. Two of the <path> tags are highlighted in blue, and their style="fill:color" parameter holds the color value that they traced in an eight-color multiple path setting.

Figure 8-15. *Review CH8_Trace_Multi_Commands.svg file SVG data*

Again Notepad can not handle all of the vector data this trace algorithm generated, so let's use Windows Explorer to see what we are getting here. As you can see, your multipath trace SVG output is 356KB, as shown at the bottom of Figure 8-16.

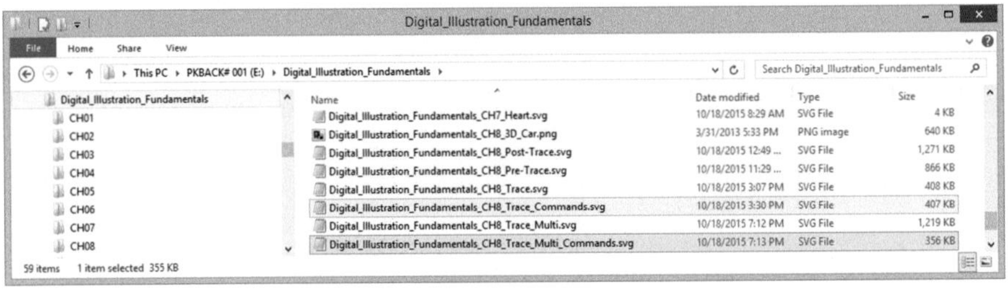

Figure 8-16. *Use the File Manager utility to compare file sizes*

A great exercise for the end of this chapter would be to put what you learned in Chapter 7 into practice and take these floating point 2.025364 six precision data values and turn them into integers, reducing eight bytes down to one. This will turn your 408KB Single Path Trace to 51KB (408KB/8), and your 356KB Multiple Path Trace to 44.5KB (356KB/8).

The best way to get familiar with the Bitmap Trace tool in Inkscape is to try all of the different settings and see if they give you the result that you are looking relative to each of your source bitmap images, because there is no way to guess what an algorithm of this complexity is going to do in every different and unique raster image vectorization scenario.

Summary

In this eighth chapter, we looked at the Inkscape **Bitmap Trace Algorithm** and how to use it properly. This is important if you ever wish to **bridge** your digital imagery into the digital illustration universe, and later, into the world of interactive application development, by using popular open source content development platforms such as Java, JavaFX, JavaScript, HTML5, Kindle, iOS, Blackberry, and Android.

In the next chapter we take a look at how to "rasterize" vector illustration in the client-side rendering engine, using the Inkscape SVG Filters menu and work process.

CHAPTER 9

■ ■ ■

The Algorithms of Digital Illustration: SVG Filters

Now that you have a solid understanding of how to apply the Inkscape Bitmap Trace Algorithm and have some experience with exporting Plain SVG XML data for further analysis, programming, or content publishing workflow, let's take a closer look at **SVG Filters** in the Inkscape Filters menu, as these can be a ton of fun to explore; and they can take your artwork to a new level!

We'll look at the Inkscape **Filters** menu, which will take the input vector illustration that you create in Inkscape, just like you did in Chapters 1 through 5, and "rasterize" it, using complex **SVG Filter algorithms** that analyze the vectors in your digital illustration and create a 2D raster image result using **SVG Filter Primitives**, which you saw in SVG XML, in Chapter 7.

SVG Filter Effects: Illustration Special FX

SVG filter effects are supported in Inkscape using the Filters menu, and its 18 submenus, yielding dozens of impressive special effects that can be applied to Scalable Vector Graphics artwork. An SVG filter effect is comprised of a series of SVG filter operations that are applied to a given source vector graphic to produce a modified image result, as you have already seen in Chapter 7, using an Inkscape spiral example. SVG Filter effects are defined with SVG filter tag elements. An SVG filter property is set on the containing (parent) tag element, or on a vector graphics element, to apply an SVG filter effect to it. Each filter element can contain a set of filter "primitives" as its children. A filter primitive performs one basic fundamental graphic operation, such as a Blend or Gaussian blur, on one or more inputs. This algorithmic processing then produces the bitmap graphic result. Most of these SVG filters represent some type of digital image algorithmic process; thus the output from these SVG filter primitives will be one 32-bit raster (bitmap) digital image using an **ARGB** format supported in Java and HTML5.

Table 9-1 shows all the SVG Filter Primitives currently supported in the **SVG Full** implementation, and which ones would be supported in the **SVG Basic** implementation. No SVG Filter is supported whatsoever in the **SVG Tiny** implementation. Thus there are three levels of SVG Filter implementation in open browsers, platforms, and devices. Be sure and check your target publishing devices, application development platforms, and browser to find out what SVG Filter implementation level it supports currently.

© Wallace Jackson 2015
W. Jackson, *Digital Illustration Fundamentals*, DOI 10.1007/978-1-4842-1697-2_9

Table 9-1. *SVG Filter Primitives*

SVG Filter Primitive	Tag Element Name	SVG Basic Support
Blend	feBlend	Yes
Color matrix	feColorMatrix	Yes
Component transfer	feComponentTransfer	Yes
Composite	feComposite	Yes
Convolve matrix	feConvolveMatrix	No
Diffuse lighting	feDiffuseLighting	No
Displacement map	feDisplacementMap	No
Flood	feFlood	Yes
Gaussian blur	feGaussianBlur	Yes
Image	feImage	Yes
Merge	feMerge	Yes
Morphology	feMorphology	No
Offset	feOffset	Yes
Specular lighting	feSpecularLighting	No
Tile	feTile	Yes
Turbulence	feTurbulence	No
Drop Shadow	feDropshadow	No

A source graphic, or the result from processing a filter primitive, can be used as an input, into one or more subsequent filter primitive processing algorithms, in a command processing infrastructure that you create using Java, JavaFX, XML or CSS3.

One application is to leverage a source graphic multiple times in your content creation, web site, eBook, or application. This is a form of data footprint optimization as only one asset needs to be transferred or stored in memory for multiple uses.

For example, an SVG filter will allow you to use a single graphic for two different assets. For instance, you could use a filter to create a monochrome copy of that source graphic, blur it using **Gaussian Blur**, offset it using **Offset** filter, and thus create a drop shadow effect. Or, you could just use the new Drop Shadow effect that was recently added to SVG Filters!

Illustration Effects: Inkscape Filters Menu

Let's get some hands-on experience with using these SVG Filters in Inkscape by using one of our recent Chapter 8 projects and applying some of the different filters to it. Open up your file you named **Digital_Illustration_Fundamentals_CH8_Trace_Multi** and drop down the **Filters** menu. You will see **18** submenus, each of which are populated from between **6** and **25** (or more) menu options. Clearly we cannot cover hundreds of SVG filter algorithms and their settings in this chapter (or book), but we can take a look at some of the more impressive and useful ones.

Bevel Effects: Using the Filters ➤ Bevel Menu

Let's take a look at the **Diffuse Light** filter in the **Bevels** menu first, as it will allow us to lighten up the image a bit and make it more presentable. As you can see, there is an ellipses, or three dots, after the filter name, as is shown in Figure 9-1. What this means is that the filter has a control panel dialog, versus the filters which do not have any dots after them, in which case they use "fixed presets" and simply apply an effect without giving you any control over the effect.

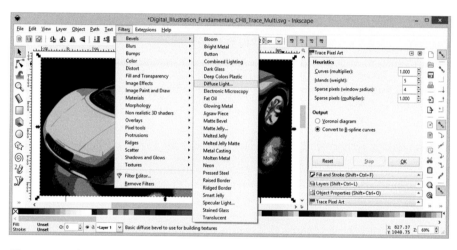

Figure 9-1. *The Filters ➤ Bevels ➤ Diffuse Light menu sequence*

As you can see in Figure 9-2, this filter allows you the ability to colorize your car, using RGBA sliders, as well as an option to **Smooth** your image, change your **Elevation** and **Azimuth**, and see a **Live Preview** of the SVG Filter effect, if you desire.

99

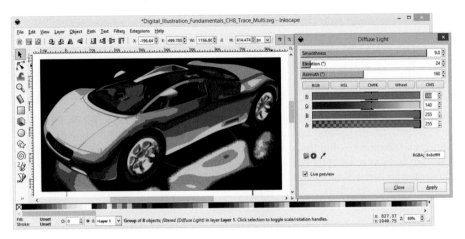

Figure 9-2. Smooth, Elevate, and Colorize the 3D Car a blue tint

I used a **Smoothness** setting of **9**, an **Elevation** setting of **24**, an **Azimuth** setting of **160**, and **RGBA** color settings of Red 140, Green 140, Blue 255, and Alpha 255, respectively.

Distortion Effects: Using the Filters ➤ Distort Menu

Next, let's take a look at the **Felt Feather** filter in the **Distort** menu, as it will allow us to apply a special effect to the edges of our 3D Car digital illustration. Applying custom edge effects to images and illustrations is a very popular thing to do these days, so this SVG Filter Effect should be quite popular with the readers. As you can see, there are ellipses, or three dots, after the filter name, as is seen in Figure 9-3, meaning that this is another filter that uses a control panel dialog. I am specifically looking at SVG Filters that utilize a dialog so that you can get experience with the more complex SVG Filters, and learn about the ones which give you the most creative control. Essentially, these customizable filters are thousands of filters inside of one configurable SVG filter, since each setting combination produces a different SVG Filter Effect. These are the most powerful SVG Filters and the ones in Inkscape that you should focus most of your time on. Select the Filters ➤ Distort ➤ Felt Feather menu sequence as is shown in Figure 9-3, and let's take a look at another powerful SVG Filter Effect available inside of Inkscape.

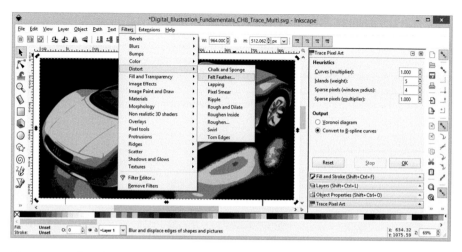

Figure 9-3. *The Filters ➤ Distort ➤ Felt Feather menu sequence*

Pull the control dialog off to the right, so you can see your source image, and then select the **Live Preview** check box on the bottom left of the dialog to show the effect in Inkscape. I used a **Type** of **Out**, **15** for Horizontal and Vertical **Blur**, **1** for **Dilatation**, zero **Erosion**, **Fractal noise Turbulence**, **Complexity** of **4**, **Variation** of **2**, **Intensity** of **50**, and **5** for Horizontal and Vertical **Frequency**. As you can see in Figure 9-4, this provides a really cool chaotic-edging special effect for the 3D car.

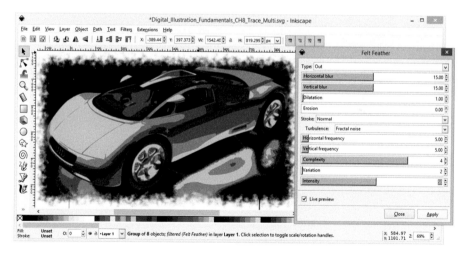

Figure 9-4. *Set Dilation, Intensity, Turbulence, and Variation*

Next, let's take a look at digital painting and drawing special effects, as we're going to start to merge digital paint into the book starting with the next chapter.

Paint and Draw Effects: Filters ➤ Paint and Draw

Let's take a look at the **Cross Engraving** filter in the **Image Paint and Draw** menu next, as it will allow us to apply those popular engraving effects to the source image, and make it more usable for special effects that require a black and white source image that has high contrast and clean edges. As you can see, this filter also has ellipses after the filter name, as shown in Figure 9-5, and it has a half dozen different options.

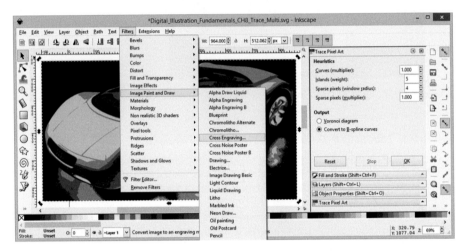

Figure 9-5. *The Filters ➤ Image Paint & Draw ➤ Cross Engraving*

I set a **Clean-up** setting of **0.5**, to provide a crisp edge and high contrast and a **Dilatation** value of **1.0**, as can be seen in Figure 9-6. In case you are wondering, Dilatation comes from the concept of dilation, like your pupils when light hits them. It literally means "the action of expanding: the state of being expanded," according to the *Merriam-Webster Dictionary*.

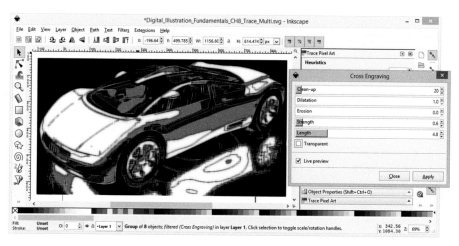

Figure 9-6. *Set CleanUp, Dilation, Strength, Erosion, and Length*

I left **Erosion** at the default value of **zero**, and set the **Strength** to **0.6**, to get exactly the effect I was looking for. A Strength is the most critical factor for this filter; you would want to use the up and down arrows to adjust this using smaller increments and look at the **Live Preview** to fine-tune the result you are looking for visually, using your finely dilated pupils.

Finally I set a **Length** value of **4.8**, to get long, strong lines in the Cross Engraving, which looks like a wood cut, only using glass. These SVG Filters provide visually cool results.

Next, let's take a look at bump mapping effects, which are usually found in 3D software, and add details to surfaces.

Bump Effects: Using the Filters ➤ Bumps Menu

Next, let's take a look at the **Wax Bump** filter in the **Bumps** menu first, as it will allow us to make our vector illustration look like it is made of dripped candle wax. Let's also change our source illustration, so close the CH8_Trace_Multi.svg and open up your **CH8_Trace.svg** file, which is shown in Figure 9-7.

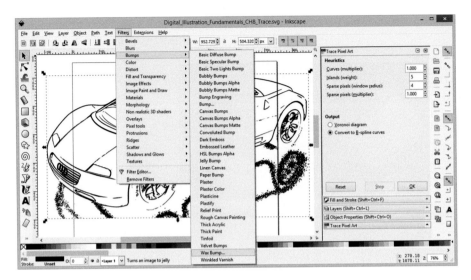

Figure 9-7. *Open up your CH8_Trace.svg Inkscape Project*

Drop down the **Filters** menu and select the **Bumps** submenu and then select the **Wax Bumps** SVG Filter Effect. Set the candle wax pink RGB color of **Red 225**, **Green 30**, and **Blue 76** in the Bump tab, as seen on the right in Figure 9-8, and select the options for **Revert Bump** and **Live Preview**. Set Transparency type to **Atop** and click the **Options** tab, to set up the Wax Bump Options next.

Figure 9-8. *Set Wax Bump options in your Bump and Options tabs*

Set your **Image Simplification** slider to a value of **1.50**, and your **Bump Simplification** slider to a value of **1.0**. Set **Crop** to 1.0 as well, and set the **Background** drop-down menu to **Color**.

Set **Background opacity** to zero, and set your **Red**, **Green**, and **Blue** sliders to **zero** as well. Finally, click on the middle **Lighting** tab, which is shown on the far-right side in Figure 9-9, to set the final collection of settings for this SVG Filter.

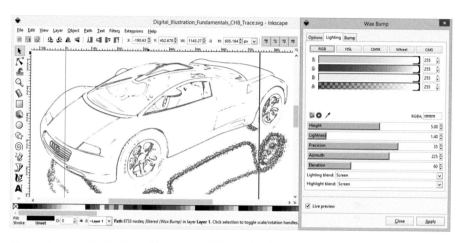

Figure 9-9. *Set the Options, Lighting, and Bump for the Wax Bump*

Set the light source to a white color by setting the RBG sliders to fully on, or a value of 255. Set the Wax Bump **Height** to a value of **5.0**, and the **Lightness** to a value of **1.40**.

Set the **Precision** value to **35**, and an **Azimuth** setting of **225**. Set your **Elevation** to **60** and set the **Lighting blend** drop-down to **Screen** and the **Highlight** blend to **Screen** as well.

You can see the Live Preview of these settings in Figure 9-9. If you like the effect, click the **Apply** button; otherwise, change these settings until you get the result that you desire.

Next, let's simulate 3D, using your Protrusion Filters!

Protrusion Effects: Using Filters ➤ Protrusions

Next, let's take a look at the **Snow crest** filter in the **Filters ➤ Protrusions** menu first, as it will allow us to accumulate snow (shaving cream?) around the edges of our 3D car. Select a **Filters ➤ Protrusions ➤ Snow crest** menu sequence, as shown in Figure 9-10. This control panel does not have many controls in it, but it at least has one, which allows you to control **drift**.

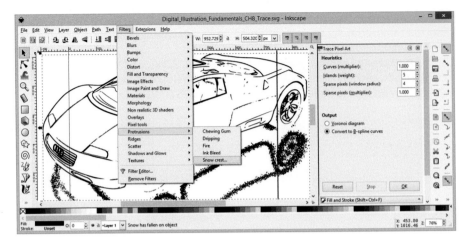

Figure 9-10. *Filters ➤ Protrustions ➤ Snow crest menu sequence*

I set a Drift Size value of 0.5 to get a compact shaving cream type of effect on and around the 3D car. Very cool stuff, as you can see in Figure 9-11.

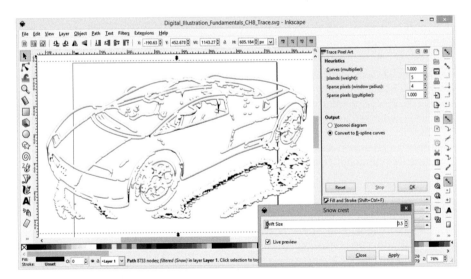

Figure 9-11. *Set Drift Size to a value of 0.5, and Live Preview*

Raster Processing: Using SVG Filters on Imagery

You don't have to only apply SVG Filters to vector imagery; you can apply it to raster imagery as well, as seen in Figure 9-12.

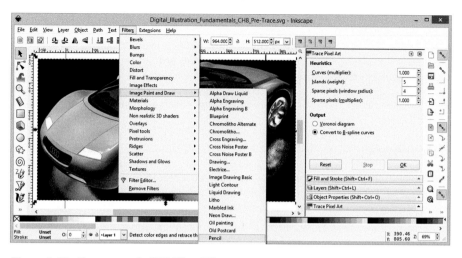

Figure 9-12. *You can apply SVG Filter Effects to source imagery*

Open your **CH8_Pre-Trace.svg** file, as is shown in Figure 9-12, and invoke a **Filters ➤ Image Paint and Draw ➤ Pencil** menu sequence. As you can see there are no ellipses after the filter name, and so your image is turned into a pencil drawing, as can be seen in Figure 9-13. This filter does a great job of turning your digital image into a pencil sketch, as you can see.

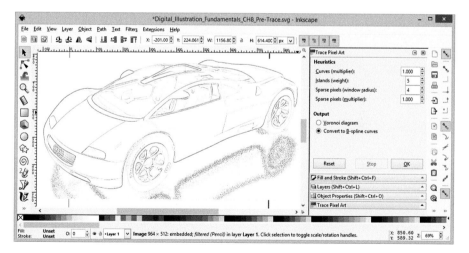

Figure 9-13. *Run the Draw ➤ Pencil filter on your CH8_Pre-Trace*

In fact, this Pencil filter works so well that you might consider using it before you run the Trace Bitmap algorithm we covered in the previous chapter to get better Bézier curve data output. Sometimes you just have to see what comes out of your work process

107

and find innovative ways to make these algorithms work in your favor as you gain more experience using them.

The best way to get familiar with the SVG Filter Effects in Inkscape is to try all of them, as well as all their various settings, and see if they give you a result that you're looking for relative to each of the source images or illustrations.

There is really no way to ascertain what an algorithm of this complexity is going to do in every different unique raster or vector image filter effect processing scenario.

Summary

In this eighth chapter, we looked at the Inkscape **SVG Filter Effects** and how to use the Effects menu. This is important if you ever wish to **bridge** digital illustration to digital images. In the next chapter, we take a look at digital painting. This will include Corel Painter 2016 and using Inkscape Brushes.

CHAPTER 10

■ ■ ■

The Progression of Digital Illustration: Painter 2016

Now that you have a good handle on vector illustration as it pertains to the SVG command syntax and SVG XML format using Inkscape, let's take a closer look at **Corel Painter 2016** and the next level in digital illustration, called digital painting in the digital illustration industry. I wanted to cover both an open source free software package as well as professional level software, so the book really takes this subject to a new level.

We'll look at how to install Corel Painter 2016, how the software differs from SVG software like Inkscape, and its main feature set. There's a Free Trial Version that you can use to follow along with during the remainder of the book if you don't want to purchase Painter 2016. This is located at: `http://www.painterartist.com/us/free-trials/` if you want to try the software out.

Corel Painter 2016: Installing the Software

Let's start with installing Corel Painter 2016, which you can get from Corel. This is one software package you'll really want to add to your content production workstation and pipeline. First you will download a **Painter 2016 x64.exe** file from Corel, then launch the installer from your browser downloads area by selecting **Run this file**, or right-clicking the EXE file and selecting **Run as Administrator**. This launches the Installer Wizard dialog, seen in Figure 10-1.

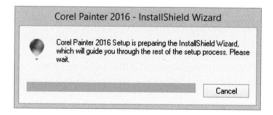

Figure 10-1. *Launch the Corel Painter 2016 InstallShield Wizard*

As you can see in Figure 10-2, once you accept a default installation location folder of **ProgramFiles/Corel/Painter2016**, you will get a **progress bar dialog** showing you the installation as it progresses.

Figure 10-2. Install to/Program Files/Corel/Painter2016 folder

Once your installation has completed, you will get this **Installation Wizard has been successful** dialog, where you will want to select your **Check for product updates** option, as shown in Figure 10-3. This will make certain that you have the latest Painter 2016 files on your multimedia production workstation.

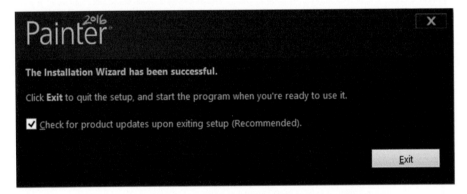

Figure 10-3. Check for product update upon exiting setup dialog

Once you click on this **Exit** button, you will get the Painter 2016 **Checking for Updates** dialog, shown on the left side in Figure 10-4. For my installation, since I have just downloaded the Painter 2016 software, this came up with the **There are no updates available at this time** dialog.

Figure 10-4. *Checking for updates dialog; click OK when updated*

After you click on the **OK** button, you can open up the OS file management utility and find your Painter executable file.

Setting Up Painter 2016: Adding Painter in Taskbar

Once you find the Painter executable file, you will then right-click on this executable and use a **Pin to Taskbar** option to create the **Quick Launch Icon** for your desktop. This is shown on the right side of Figure 10-5 in the context-sensitive menu, where you can **Pin to Start** (Menu), or Pin to Taskbar (or both).

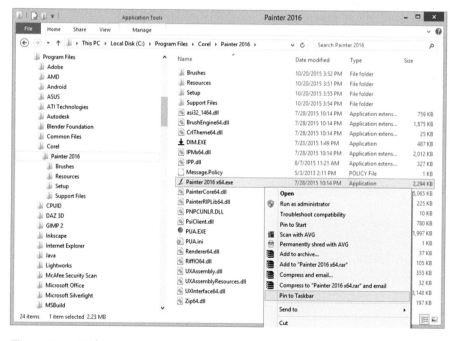

Figure 10-5. *Find Painter2016x64.exe right-click Pin to Taskbar*

Once you have a Quick Launch Icon, you can then click on it anytime to launch Painter 2016. Let's do that now. You will get the Painter 2016 startup screen, as shown in Figure 10-6.

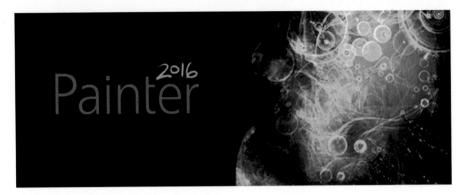

Figure 10-6. *Click the QuickLaunch Icon in TaskBar to launch it*

Once Painter 2016 starts you'll then get a control panel seen in Figure 10-7 where you can learn Painter or get content.

Figure 10-7. *The Painter 2016 Startup Screen's User Interface*

I like to leave the Show this at startup option selected so that I always have the Painter 2016 control panel available to me, in case I ever need it later on for any reason.

If you do not select anything inside the startup control panel, a time-out will eventually bring up the **New Image** dialog automatically, so that you can create a new image to work on. I named mine **Digital_Painting_CH10**, as you can see in Figure 10-8 and accepted the default values for the new image dialog.

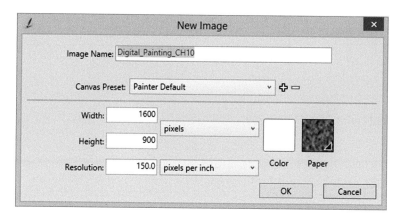

Figure 10-8. *A New Image dialog shows after Start-Up times out*

Next, let's take a look at how to install Painter **Brush Packs**, which allow you to add powerful tools to Painter 2016.

Enhancing Painter 2016: Installing Brush Packs

Corel offers something called Painter Brush Packs so you can enhance your Painter 2016 installation with some additional physics-based brush settings, which we will introduce you to in this chapter, and cover in greater detail during Chapter 11. We will take a closer look at how to create your own custom brush; however Painter artists have spent a lot of time creating these Brush Pack collections of custom brushes, which can save you a ton of time doing this on your own, and allows you to get right down to creating your digital painting artwork.

If you purchased and downloaded any of these Corel Brush Packs, you probably downloaded them to the same folder location as the Painter2016x64.exe file. In my case this was a C:/Painter2016 folder, which is shown on the right side of Figure 10-9.

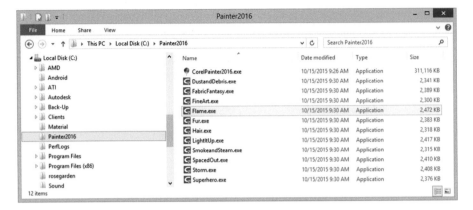

Figure 10-9. If you have any custom brushes, install them next

As you can see I downloaded 11 of the Corel Brush Packs, allowing me to enhance Painter 2016 with powerful **physics-based brush engines** to enhance my creativity by an order of magnitude allowing me to get to the actual client project workflow rather than building the digital painting brush tools that I will need to create those client deliverables.

Next, let's install one of these Brush Packs, to see how they all would be installed. Double-click on your DustandDebris installer EXE, or any of the Brush Packs that you have decided to purchase and download, and launch the installation process.

Your first dialog will be an **Extracting** dialog, shown on the left side in Figure 10-10. Next, you should get the **License Agreement** dialog, where you need to accept a license agreement.

Figure 10-10. Launch Installer Wizard, and accept the agreement

After you click on the **Install** button, which is shown in the middle of Figure 10-10, you will get an **Installing** progress bar dialog, shown on the right side of Figure 10-10.

Next, let's launch Painter 2016 and make sure that it is working, and take a look at the primary areas in Painter's user interface, which are located at the top of the software as well as in draggable palettes that dock into place at the sizes and bottom of the screen, as you can see in Figure 10-11. There are only three floating palettes, six panes with tabs, two floating toolbars, and one drop-down Brushes selector open in the default Painter 2016 configuration. I pasted part of the Window menu in the middle of the screen, to show some of the other palette and tab options you can open in Painter, some of which are shown in Figure 10-12. As you can see, Painter is quite a complex piece of software.

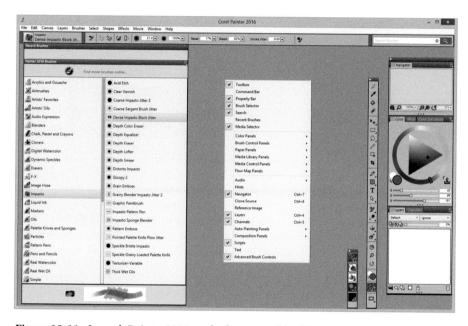

Figure 10-11. *Launch Painter 2016, and take a tour of its GUI*

Now that we know Painter works, let's take a look at how it approaches digital illustration. We'll take a tour of the UI to get a closer look at the complexity lurking under the hood.

Painter 2016: Vectors, Rasters, and Advanced Code

Corel Painter started out decades ago as Fractal Design Painter as a competitor to CorelDRAW, which was the first software to combine vector illustration and raster imaging into one unified program. Corel acquired Painter, and this latest 2016 version combines vector, raster, and algorithms, simulating **painting** using raster **brushes**, along vector **strokes**. Painter's algorithms control how the brushes react to strokes.

The best way to take a look at what Painter offers is to take a look at **tools**, **palettes**, **panes** (or **tabs**) that it offers, which can be seen in Figure 10-12. The Painter canvas is always shown using a blue window border, whereas the rest of the UI is in grayscale. Brushes are always available at the top left, and settings for the currently selected brush, are along the top.

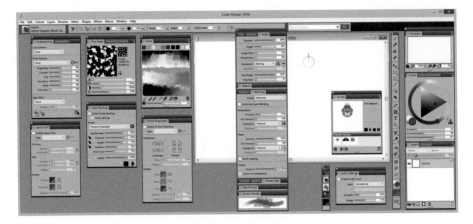

Figure 10-12. *Showing some of the powerful floating palettes*

Starting at the left, your **Underpainting** and **Restoration** panes are used for advanced photographic image restoration, and will be covered in my *Digital Painting Techniques* title (Apress, 2015). These allow you to restore or enhance your digital image and digital painting assets. The **Layout Grid** pane allows you to create grid layout guidelines for your digital painting content creation work process. The next two over are **Flow Maps** and **Auto Painting**, which allow control over how the brush imagery reacts to the **stroke dynamics** (from the hardware tablet, and pressure-sensitive stylus). The next two over are an organic paint **Mixer** pane and the Divine Proporation pane, which allows you to paint based on the Fibonacci spiral found in nature by harnessing the complex Fibonacci algorithms built right into Painter. The tall palette shown selected (blue outline) in Figure 10-12, which has several panes docked into in, including the **Size, Color, Angle, Spacing, Impasto, Blending,** and **Stroke Jitter**, has more controls over how your Painter Brush will react to your stroke dynamics.

The next two smaller palettes, and smaller toolbar, will allow access to custom **Scripts** and real-time **Audio Settings** for brush stroke dynamics (floating panes), and access to different **patterns, gradients, nozzles, weaves,** and **brush looks** (floating toolbar). Nozzles allow you to paint with images along strokes.

We'll get into Brushes and Nozzles in greater detail in Chapter 11. The Primary **Painter Toolbar**, seen on the right side of Figures 10-2 and 10-3, holds your tools that you'll be using to create your digital paintings with. The three palettes to the right of that are a **Navigator**, allowing you to navigate, or scroll around large paintings, the **Color** wheel and swatches, and **Layers** and **Channels**, which we will be learning about during Chapter 12, covering using multiple layers, to create **composite** digital illustration assets, content, and artwork.

Finally I added Figure 10-13 to show you how to find the Brush Packs that you installed earlier in the chapter, as they are not readily evident in the user interface. To locate these, drop down the Painter Brushes navigator at the top left of your Painter 2016 software, scroll the left pane down to the bottom, and you will find the Brush Packs there, shown in Figure 10-13.

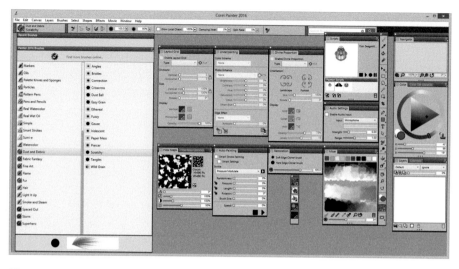

Figure 10-13. *Ensure Brush Pack you installed is on Brush menu*

Summary

In this tenth chapter, to take a short break from Inkscape, we installed and looked at a professional illustration software package from Corel called **Painter 2016**. I did this so that over the next few advanced chapters, covering things such as **brushes** and **layers**, we could look at an open source software package as well as a professional software package, just like I do in my *Digital Image Compositing Fundamentals* title (Apress, 2015). We will look at brushes in greater detail during the next chapter.

CHAPTER 11

■ ■ ■

The Airbrush of Digital Illustration: Using Brushes

Now that you have both Inkscape 0.91 and **Corel Painter 2016** on your digital illustration workstation and have learned about the next level in digital illustration called digital painting, I want to cover the topic of using brushes, in both your open source free software package, as well as for professional-level software, so that we can keep covering more advanced topics as this book progresses.

We will look at how to implement Inkscape brush strokes, which is surprisingly robust at digital painting for an SVG XML generation software package, as well as in Corel Painter, which is focused more on digital painting than digital illustration.

Inkscape Brush Strokes: Digital Painting

Inkscape hasn't put an emphasis on brush-based digital painting in the way that Corel Painter has, as you can tell in Figure 11-1, by noticing the **fountain pen** that is currently being used for the Inkscape **Draw Calligraphic or Brush Strokes** tool. That being said, there are still a dozen different settings for your brush stroke design work process as well as a Presets drop-down where you can store cool brushes, or use the ones that Inkscape offers, so Inkscape is making steady progress in the area of digital painting. What is even more significant in Inkscape's ongoing support of digital painting is that there are a few icon toggles that specifically support digital painting tablet hardware settings such as stylus pressure and stylus angle, so anyone who tells you Inkscape isn't supporting or focusing on brush strokes and digital painting needs to take a look at the Inkscape 0.91 Draw Brush Strokes Setting Bar at the top of the software, which can be seen in Figure 11-1 and which we will be looking at in detail in this first section of the chapter.

© Wallace Jackson 2015

W. Jackson, *Digital Illustration Fundamentals*, DOI 10.1007/978-1-4842-1697-2_11

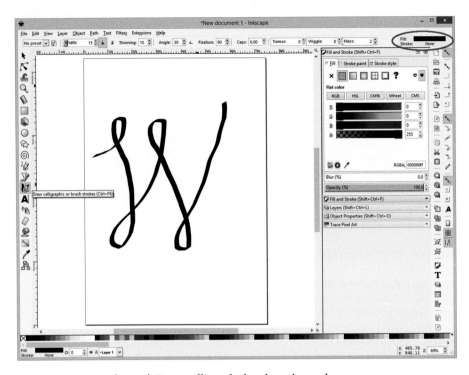

Figure 11-1. *Use Inkscape's Draw calligraphy brush strokes tool*

Calligraphy Brush Stroke Tool: Basic Style Setting

Open Inkscape and select a Calligraphic and Brush Stroke tool from the toolbar, and draw brush strokes on your canvas.

As you can see in Figure 11-1, you can click on **Fill** and **Stroke** indicators, at the far right of the **Brush Stroke Setting Bar** at the top of Inkscape, to configure the style of the brush stroke, which I set to be a black magic marker effect, for now.

Click your Fill and Stroke indicator color bars, circled in red on the right-hand side of Figure 11-1, and bring up your **Preferences ➤ Calligraphy** dialog, which is shown in Figure 11-2.

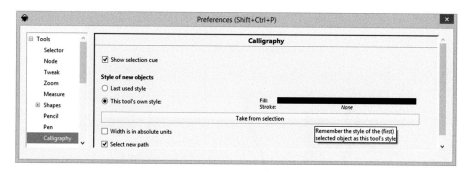

Figure 11-2. *Set Brush Stroke Calligraphy in Preferences dialog*

I checked the **Show selection cue** and the **Select new path** tool helper options, as you can see, and I set the **Style of new objects** option to **This tool's own style**. You can set these Fill and Stroke indicators on the right by using a button underneath them labeled "Take from selection," which copies the style from a selection. You can also set these style characteristics for a brush stroke by selecting the stroke after you lay it down. The reason I set my brush tool to black is so I can see it better.

I created a loopy W, using the Brush Strokes tool, shown in Figure 11-1 and 11-3, and then selected it and left the Fill as Black, and I set the **Stroke style** to **2 pixels** and the **Stroke paint** to a magenta value by using an RGB color value of Red 216 (85%), Green zero, and Blue 216 (85%). I copied and then pasted the Stroke style dialog over the canvas to show these settings.

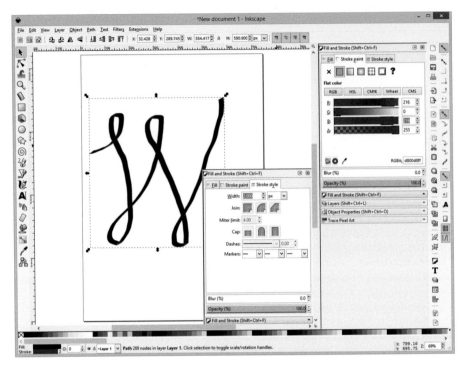

Figure 11-3. *Style brush stroke in Stroke Style or Stroke Paint*

Now that we have covered the basics of stroke colors and styling, let's take a look at the stroke dynamics settings that allow Inkscape to do at least some of what Painter 2016 does in the digital painting realm of digital illustration workflows.

Brush Stroke Configuration: Advanced Settings

If you don't want to design custom Inkscape brush stroke dynamics configurations, which is what you'll be learning about in this section, you can use brush stroke presets, shown on the left side in Figure 11-4, in the brush drop-down menu selector.

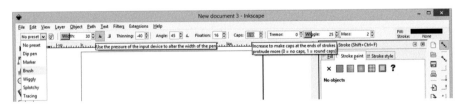

Figure 11-4. *Brush Stroke presets, stylus pressure, and Caps*

Also shown, selected in blue, on the left side of Figure 11-4, is the "Use the pressure of the input device to alter the width of the pen" option toggle icon, which allows Inkscape the ability to use your digital painting tablet or stylus hardware.

Also shown selected in blue, and with the yellow tooltip pop-up helper message showing, is the **Caps** spinner. This allows you to make the "caps" at the end of the brush strokes protrude more than they otherwise should. Use caps for a visual painting guide to help you lay down the brush strokes you want to paint.

There's another feature toggle icon, seen on the left in Figure 11-5, which automates a tracing process by looking at the background contrast (light versus dark) and adjusting the brush width to match pixel contrast (darkness), making traces easier.

Figure 11-5. *The Trace lightness, Fixation, and Mass settings*

The **Mass** setting, shown on the right side of the screen, adds mass to your brush stroke, which makes the pen drag behind the stroke the higher the value you set, the more drag you get.

In physics, mass allows an object to have inertia. The higher you set the Mass setting for Inkscape's calligraphy tool, the more it will "smooth out" sharp turns and quick jerks in your brush strokes. The default value (of 2) for the setting is initially set small so that the tool is fast and responsive, but you can increase this Mass and get a slower and smoother pen.

The **fixation** parameter, shown highlighted in Figure 11-5 in blue in the middle of the screen, controls a level of stroke contrast between thin and thick strokes based on stylus angle.

A fixation value of 0 means that a brush angle is always constant, and so the stroke will be uniform no matter what the stylus angle. This could be said to give the least calligraphic effect and so you'll get a very non-calligraphic stroke, as can be seen in Figure 11-1, where we have a very low setting of 16.

A fixation value of 100 means that a brush stroke should rotate freely, resulting in a stroke perpendicular to the stylus, like a fountain pen. This results in an exaggerated calligraphy stroke, as can be seen in Figure 11-6, where I used a very high-fixation setting of 100, shown circled in red at the top of the screen.

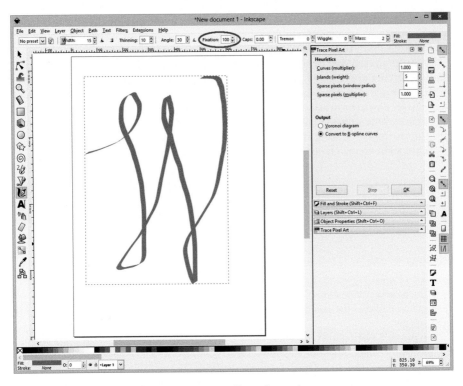

Figure 11-6. *A fixation setting of 100 gives calligraphy stroke*

Decreasing a fixation value allows your calligraphic pen to turn less and less relative to the direction of your stroke.

The third feature toggle icon, which has what looks like a protractor on it, can be seen in blue in the middle of Figure 11-7. This turns on your tablet stylus hardware's **tilt** feature. If you turn this on the Angle spinner is grayed-out, as you can see, because the tilt of your stylus is controlling this value.

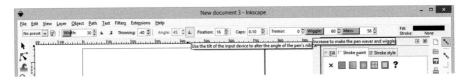

Figure 11-7. *Stylus tilt toggle icon and Wiggle slider setting*

The Wiggle slider controls the waver and "wiggle" of the brush stroke, and is akin to the resistance of the paper to the movement of your stylus (or mouse). The default is set to zero, the minimum value possible, and increasing this parameter makes your canvas surface (paper) more and more slippery. If the Mass setting is a high data value, your stylus will tend to run away when sharp turns are implemented. If your Mass setting is zero, high wiggle values will make brush strokes wiggle erratically.

The last two settings, shown selected in blue and with a tooltip pop-up deployed in Figure 11-8, are a **Thinning** spinner and a **Tremor** slider. The Tremor setting is there to control the slight wavering, common with calligraphy strokes. Tremor ranges from 0 to 100, producing anything from slight unevenness (1–16) to wild blotches and splotches (80–100). A proper use of Tremor will significantly expand your creative use of the Brush tool.

Figure 11-8. *The Thinning spinner setting and the Tremor slider*

If you set the Thinning parameter to a nonzero value, a brush stroke width would vary with velocity, controlled by this Thinning parameter. The parameter value ranges from 100 to 100 with positive values making rapid strokes thinner, and negative values making rapid strokes broader. The default value is **0.10** and implement a very moderate thinning of fast brush strokes.

Painter 2016 Brushes: Dynamic Painting

As amazing as it is that Inkscape has a brush stroke tool that uses pressure and tilt sensitive stylus and table hardware, and therefore will allow digital painting to be performed with open source software, there's a paid software package that is taking digital painting to new levels year after year, with the latest Painter 2016 version released just in time for me to be able to include coverage of this latest digital painting technology for this book. I will also be writing a Digital Painting Techniques title for Apress during the last two months of 2015 that should be available from Apress sometime in the last quarter of 2015.

Manual Painting: Using Painter's Cloning Feature

One of the most popular work processes in Painter is using an image as a guide for brush color, which is taken from a source image and then painted by the user onto a cloned image canvas. I will show you this work process first, and then later take a look at Auto-Painting where you can have Painter 2016 do all of the work for you. The first thing that you will need to do, as you can see in Figure 11-9, is to open a source image that you want to create a digital painting out of using the **File ➤ Open** menu sequence. Find the **Niki.png** image in the book repository and open it. This Niki image is a PNG24 from my *Digital Image Compositing* (Apress, 2015) title, which I wrote earlier this year, about the Adobe Photoshop CS6 and GIMP 2.8 image editors.

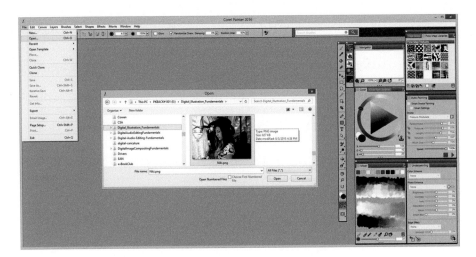

Figure 11-9. *Use File ➤ Open and select a Niki.png source image*

The next step is to use your **File ➤ Clone** menu sequence, which is shown on the left-hand side of Figure 11-10. This will "clone" the original source image that you opened up first, and you can then paint on top of it, or edit it in any way that you wish, or even fill it with solid color, so as to create a blank canvas. Painter has so many different options, it will blow your mind, and mastering it over the next few years should be fun!

Figure 11-10. *Use File ➤ Clone to create a clone image to paint*

The next step will be to select the original Niki source image, shown on the right side in Figure 11-11, and then select the **Dropper** tool icon, shown circled in red with an oval on the right side of the screen shot in the Painter primary toolbar.

Figure 11-11. *Use the Dropper tool to select a cream background*

Using the Dropper tool, select a color from the Niki.png source image to use as a background color. I liked that vanilla ice cream color, in the ceiling panels. I circled the area that I selected the color from in red, in Figure 11-11, so you could see where I clicked the Dropper tool to select the color value.

Once you select the fill color it will set the **Color** tab and its color wheel widget in Painter to display that particular color value, in this case, this is **Red 229**, **Green 214**, and **Blue 191**, as you can see on the right side in Figure 11-11.

Now you have a nice creamy background color that you can set for your cloned image that you will be painting on with the source image pixel color values going to the paint brush engine algorithm.

Since Painter 2016 is "modal," like Photoshop, and GIMP, you'll have to select the cloned window before you do the Fill.

Next select the cloned image window, which is currently named **Untitled-2**, until we do the Save As in the next step and rename this Chapter-11-Brushes.riff. Use your **Edit ➤ Fill** menu sequence, which is shown on the left side in Figure 11-12, and fill this window with the cream color. This will paint over and obscure the image data that has been cloned (copied) from your source Niki.png PNG24 digital image that you opened or imported into Painter 2016.

Figure 11-12. *Fill your clone image using the Edit ➤ Fill menu*

Once you invoke this Edit ➤ Fill menu sequence, you will get the Fill dialog where you can use the **Current Color** (crème) **Fill with:** setting from the drop-down menu, and set an Opacity, if you like, to cross-fade the fill color with the cloned image pixel color values. I used the **Opacity** value of **100%**.

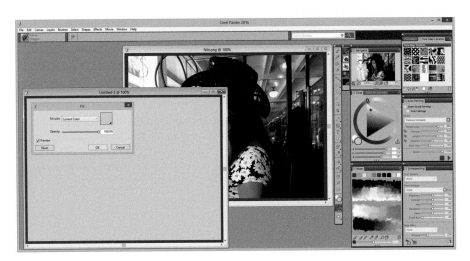

Figure 11-13. *Select Fill with: Current Color and Opacity: 100%*

Before I started this clone painting process, I used the File ➤ Save As menu sequence, seen in Figure 11-13, and I saved the file as **Chapter-11-Brushes.rif** (or .riff, for Mac OS X).

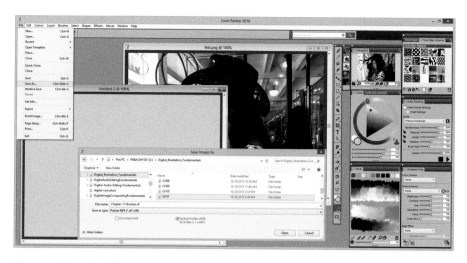

Figure 11-14. *Use File* ➤ *Save As and save as Chapter-11-Brushes*

Next, drop down the Painter Brushes selector in the top left of the Painter user interface and select the **Cloners** group from the left side of the drop-down UI selector, as is shown in Figure 11-15. I selected a Painter **Chalk Cloner 2** brush, whose preview can be seen at the bottom of the drop-down selector UI.

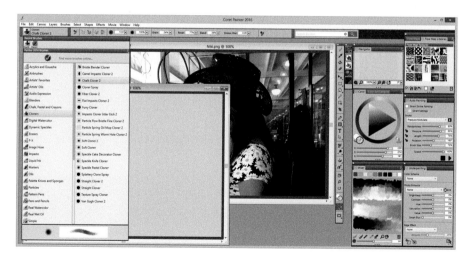

Figure 11-15. *Select the Cloners Brush Group and Chalk Cloner 2*

Next I selected a fairly fine brush size value of 10, as this will give me more detail in the resulting painting. Figure 11-16 shows this setting, circled in red at the top, as well as some of my brush strokes that I started in the facial area, so that you can see how the details can come through in the paint!

Figure 11-16. *Set Brush Size to 10 and paint in the facial area*

Automatic Painting: Using Painter's Auto-Painting

Next I am going to show you how to have Painter 2016 do all the digital painting work for you, using the **Auto-Painting** floating palette in conjunction with the **Underpainting** floating palette. You would start this work process the same way that you did in Figure 11-9, but instead of using a File ➤ Clone menu sequence, use a **File ➤ Quick Clone** menu sequence, which is shown in Figure 11-17.

Figure 11-17. *This time, use a File ➤ Quick Clone menu sequence*

This will open an auto-clone window, which I saved using a **Chapter-11-Auto-Paint.rif** file name. It also opens your **Clone Source** floating palette with **Niki** in it, shown in Figure 11-18.

Figure 11-18. *Clone Source floating palette appears showing PNG*

Next, drop down the Painter Brushes selector, and select the **Smart Strokes** Group, and select a **Watercolor Spatter Water** brush from the right side of your drop-down menu, as is seen in Figure 11-19. There is a preview of what a brush will look like located at the bottom of the Painter Brushes drop-down selector user interface, so you can preview the effect of these brushes.

Figure 11-19. *Select Smart Strokes* ➤ *Watercolor Spatter Water*

To get Painter 2016 to create a digital painting for you automatically, click on the **Play** button I circled in Figure 11-19, until you get the result that you wanted. After that, click on the **Stop** button, shown highlighted in blue, in Figure 11-20.

Figure 11-20. *Click Play and Stop icons to control Auto-Paint*

As you have seen during this chapter, Painter 2016 is an extremely advanced algorithmic digital painting engine, which a producer will need to put in years of practice to master.

If you want to create original artwork for your clients, it will be well worth your time and a lot of fun to explore in that process anyway, so I suggest mastering this powerful paint and illustration software and then adding it to your multimedia content production tool set.

Summary

In this eleventh chapter, we covered using brushes and brush strokes in both Inkscape as well as the digital painting and illustration software package from Corel called **Painter 2016**. We looked at the Inkscape Calligraphic and Brush Stoke tool and its settings in the first half of the chapter, and then we looked at manual digital painting using Clone in Painter, and automatic digital painting using the Quick Clone work process after that. We will look at layers and channels and digital image and painting and illustration compositing in greater detail during Chapter 12.

■ ■ ■

The Compositing of Digital Illustration: Using Layers

Now that you have learned how to use brushes using brush strokes with tablet and stylus hardware to create digital painting artwork in digital illustration software packages, the next logical step would be to learn how to leverage your Layers Palette to organize your digital illustration projects. A layer allows you to isolate components of your artwork, as well as to apply special imaging effects, such as those provided using SVG Filters covered in Chapter 7, to individual layers. The process of using multiple layers (rather than just one, called the base or **background** layer) to create a complex composition is called "compositing" and was first offered in digital imaging software packages such as Adobe Photoshop, Corel PaintShop Pro, and GIMP.

Originally, in early digital imaging software revisions, layers just isolated **masked** objects, like vellum on an overhead projector allows you to add to your presentations. The layer was designed to hold image compositing components, but at a certain point in the development cycle, developers started adding other cool features to layers, making them an order of magnitude more powerful. We will be learning about **masking** and **alpha channels** palettes during this chapter as well, as they are intertwined. In fact, we will also be covering some digital imaging concepts that also apply to digital painting or digital illustration.

Painter and Inkscape have a stable of layer organization tools, which can be used to organize very complex digital paint or digital illustration compositing pipeline, or special effect pipeline construct. In fact, layers are the reason for the term "pipeline" as they allow you to construct a series of moves or algorithms together, to control the processing of your artwork.

You'll be learning all about Inkscape and Painter layers during the course of this chapter. Let's get started; we have a lot to cover! Layers and layers of relevant layers information are contained in this chapter, in fact; and no pun is intended!

Alpha Channels: Defining Transparency

Since each layer contains an alpha channel that defines the transparent areas (or it wouldn't be able to be used as a layer), let's take a look at how alpha channels define digital image, painting or illustration pixel transparency values, and how layers and their channels are used for compositing digital illustration and digital painting content. Each layer will need

© Wallace Jackson 2015
W. Jackson, *Digital Illustration Fundamentals*, DOI 10.1007/978-1-4842-1697-2_12

to support an alpha channel to define what will be seen on that layer and what should show through on the layers underneath it.

Alpha channels provide transparency support in different digital content production software, as well as in your content publishing platforms, such as HTML5, Java, JavaFX, Android, EPUB3, Kindle, and the like, which I will be covering in the final two chapters of the book covering programming and publishing.

Layer Compositing: Complex Alpha-based Pipeline

Digital **layer compositing** always involves the **seamless blending** together of more than one layer of digital painting, and as you might imagine, **per pixel transparency** is an extremely important concept. Digital layer compositing is used from graphic design, to feature film, to 3D game design, to digital illustration and digital painting, to interactive applications development.

Digital layer compositing needs to be used when you want to create "content" on the display that appears as though it is one single image (or illustration) but is actually the seamless collection of more than one composited artwork layer.

One of the principle reasons you will set up your image, illustration, painting, video, or animation composition, should be to give you precise control over various elements in digital layer compositing software such as Painter, Inkscape, Photoshop, and GIMP. This is done by having artwork components isolated by using layers to allow you to position, blend, rotate, translate (move or animate), and apply special effects to individual paint or illustration (or imaging) artwork composition components.

Channel Data: Red, Green, Blue, and Alpha Channel

To accomplish multilayer compositing you always need to have an **alpha channel transparency value**, which you can utilize to precisely control the **blending** of the pixel's color with the pixels in the same X,Y image location on other layers below it. Like the **RGB** color channels, alpha channels can have **256 levels** of transparency, ranging from **100%transparent**, to **100%opaque**. You saw this early on in this book in Chapter 3, in Figure 3-3.

Each pixel in a digital illustration, digital painting, digital image, or digital video composition will have different alpha transparency data, just as each pixel will have different Red, Green, or Blue color data values associated with the pixel.

You saw during Chapter 6, in Figure 6-5, that your alpha channel transparency data values are shown for each pixel using a **checkerboard pattern**. This convention is the same for digital imaging, digital illustration, digital painting, digital video, and even application development environments such as IntelliJ, Android Studio, NetBeans (Java, JavaFX, and HTML5), and Eclipse.

Masking: Using Alpha Channel Data for Selections

Alpha channels aren't only used for defining transparent areas in your compositing pipeline (layer stack); they can also be used for more creative purposes, such as storing **selections**. As you observed in Figure 6-5, I have the heart element I created in an

Inkscape digital illustration software package on its own layer, seamlessly and perfectly defined using the alpha channel data. All digital content composition software, whether it is for imaging, painting, illustration, or video, will contain layer command (tool) options for selecting the RGB color data in the RGB channels using the alpha channel transparency data values in the A channel, when 32-bit RGBA support is available.

This is the primary use, in fact, for the PNG32 image file format, as the format needs to carry the object's selection set data in the alpha channel. Once this PNG32 is imported into one of your digital compositing genres mentioned above, the "select using alpha channel values" work process will then allow you to extract the RGB pixels for only your intended object (element), allowing for a layer-based compositing pipeline implementation.

This RGBA support you will find in all digital composite (layer) capable multimedia content production genres allows you to "bridge" these genres together using alpha channel selection capable, PNG32 RGBA format. Let's bridge a digital illustration with the Niki.png digital image that I used in Chapter 11, next.

Using Masked Imagery: A Simple Layer Composite

Let's use GIMP again, and open up your PolkaHeartStroke.png image, using the GIMP **File ➤ Open** menu sequence. As you can see in Figure 12-1, you can either right-click on a layer to select the **Alpha to Selection** menu option, or, you can click the **Fuzzy Select Tool**, seen selected in blue at the top right, and select its "select transparent areas" option, which is seen circled in red, in the middle of the right-hand side of this screenshot.

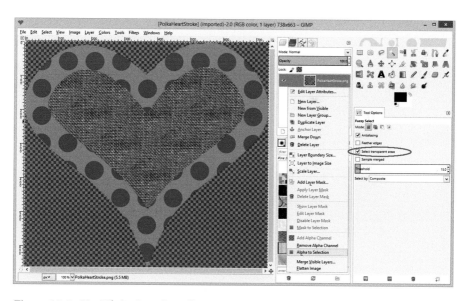

***Figure 12-1.** Use File ➤ Open ➤ PolkaHeartStroke.png in GIMP 2.8*

135

Next, use the **File ➤ Open as Layers** menu sequence, as is shown in Figure 12-2, and create a composite, using this heart.

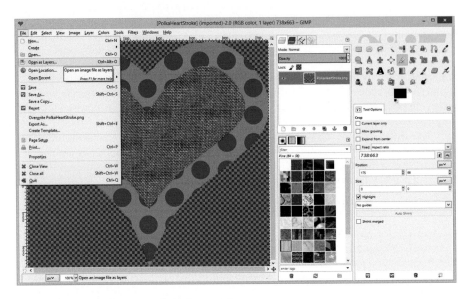

Figure 12-2. *Use the GIMP File ➤ Open as Layers menu sequence*

Use the GIMP **Open Image** dialog, shown in Figure 12-3, to open the **Niki.png** digital image included with the book (it's in the book repository on the Apress.com web site).

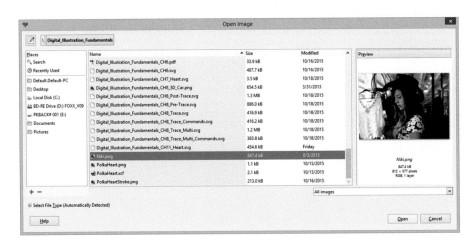

Figure 12-3. *Find the Niki.png image, and click the Open button*

Next, right-click on the Niki.png layer, shown in Figure 12-4 in blue, and select the **Scale Layer** context-sensitive menu option, so that you can scale the Niki image to match the heart object. This can be seen behind Niki, at the top of the Figure.

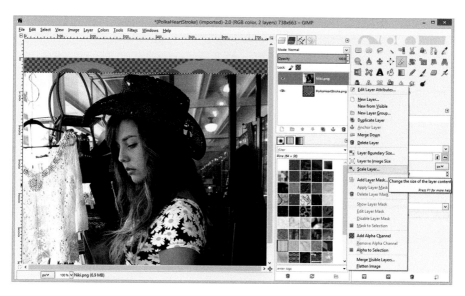

Figure 12-4. *Select Niki.png layer, right-click, and Scale Layer*

In the **Scale Layer** dialog, as seen in Figure 12-5, along with the scaled Niki layer result of this operation, set **Height** to a value of **663**, which is the height of your Heart object. As you can see I kept the aspect ratio (shape of the image) locked for the scaling operation by not clicking on a **chain** connection icon, which is connecting the Width and Height fields together.

Figure 12-5. *Set Height value to 663; use a Cubic Interpolation*

Use the **Cubic Interpolation** setting for the best quality image scaling result, and finally, click on the **Scale** button.

Notice that I added a Scale Layer dialog to this imaging composite, so that I could show both the Scale Layer dialog, as well as the scaled Niki.png image result, that this dialog will provide to you once you click on the Scale button.

As you can see, the Niki.png layer is now obscuring your PolkaHeartStroke.png layer, so we have a problem. Since this is the chapter on layers, let's learn a little bit about layers in GIMP, since at this fundamental level, layers work the same for digital imaging, digital videos, digital illustrations, digital painting, and most of the content development platforms as well.

Layer order greatly affects a compositing pipeline; thus any layer without transparency, such as a PNG24 Niki.png image, needs to be on the bottom layer of the layer stack. PNG32 image assets such as the PolkaHeartStroke.png file need to be on top of the stack, so their alpha channel transparency is calculated by your layer compositing engine (algorithms in your software).

Changing layer order in content production software will always be as simple as clicking on one layer and dragging it to the desired position above or below the other layer, to reorder the layers in your composite. Let's try this, using GIMP, next.

In this case, we will drag the Niki.png layer down under the PolkaHeartStroke.png layer, and as is shown in Figure 12-6, the heart is now on top of the Niki image. So that this model's face is not obscured, I selected the **PolkaHeartStroke.png** layer by clicking on it, and then I set the **Opacity** slider on the top of the **Layers palette** to a value of **50%**.

Figure 12-6. *Drag Niki layer under Heart and set Opacity to 50%*

It is important to notice that since we are using a Fill pattern in the middle of the heart object that uses grayscale, and not color like the Stroke element does, that the color data from your Niki.png image layer, behind the digital illustration layer, is preserved.

This makes it look like you are implementing a texturing special effect over the image data, which now shows through the center portion of the heart object with correct Hue color value and with lightness values that are changed via the **50% Opacity** blending, implemented by the **Layer Opacity** setting slider bar.

Since we are covering Inkscape and Painter 2016 for this book, let's spend the rest of the chapter specifically looking at the layer functionality for both of these software packages. You will find there are a lot of similarities, where layers are concerned, among digital new media content production tools.

Inkscape Layers: Illustration Compositing

Now let's switch from Digital Image Compositing software (GIMP) to Digital Illustration Compositing software (Inkscape). Later, we will also cover a Digital Painting and Compositing software package (Painter 2016), so three different genres of multimedia production software will be covered in one single chapter. We will first take a look at how to set a background transparency, or a background color of white (or any other color), since your CH6 project already features a default transparent background. After that we will add several layers to the Chapter 6 project.

Inkscape Document Alpha Channel: Transparency

To set the document transparency for your Inkscape project, use the **File ➤ Document Properties** menu sequence, as is seen on the left side of Figure 12-7.

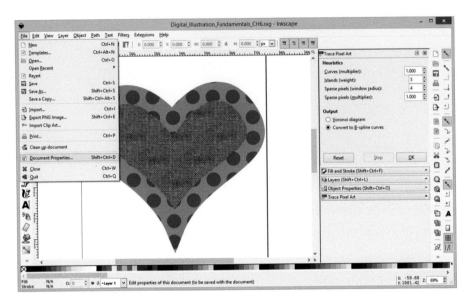

Figure 12-7. *The Painter 2016 Start-Up Screen's User Interface*

This will bring up your multi-tabbed Document Properties dialog, as you can see in Figure 12-8, and tabs to set property preferences for your Page, Guides, Grids, Snap, Color, Scripts, Metadata, and Licensing. Select the **Page** tab, as shown in Figure 12-8, and at the bottom, click on your **Background color swatch**, which will open a **Background color** dialog with the color picker in it. To set Page Color to **White**, set your **Alpha** value to **255**.

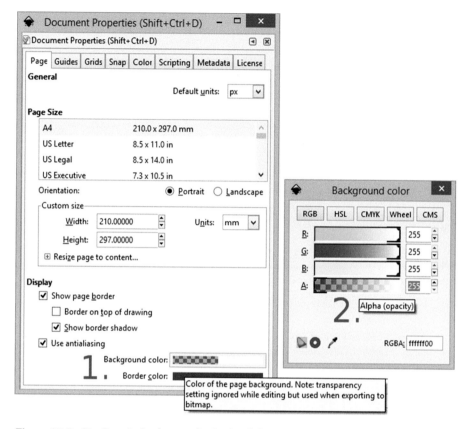

Figure 12-8. *Use Page ➤ background color ➤ Alpha to set transparency*

Next, let's take a look at how to use the Inkscape Layer tab to add Text objects to your Heart project to create a cool Valentine's Day card for your significant other.

Complex Illustration Compositing: Layers Palette

Next let's increase the complexity of your Chapter 6 project, and add some layers containing other objects, to take this to a new and more functional level. Open your CH6.svg project file, and let's create a greeting card on top of the current artwork. The first thing you will learn is how to rename a layer, so double-click on the Layer 1 label and type in Heart_Object, as is seen on the right side of Figure 12-9. Click on the **plus (+) icon** at the bottom left and use the **Add Layer** dialog to add the **Layer name: happy_Text_Object**. Select a **Position: Above current** drop-down menu setting, and then click on the **Add** button.

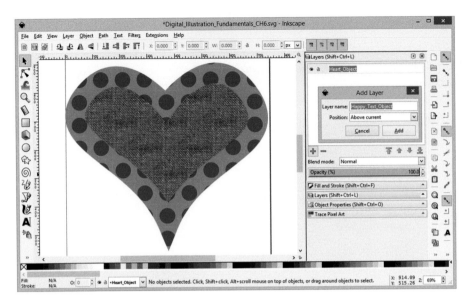

Figure 12-9. *Name the Heart_Object layer; Add Happy_Text layer*

Next, add a **Brush Script Text** object, as shown in Figure 12-10, and then add another layer named **Valentines_Text_Object**.

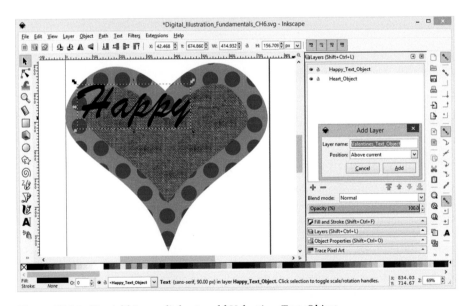

Figure 12-10. *Use Add Layer dialog to add Valentine_Text_Object*

Next, add a **Sans Serif Text** object, as is seen in Figure 12-11, and then add a final layer and name it **Day_Text_Object**.

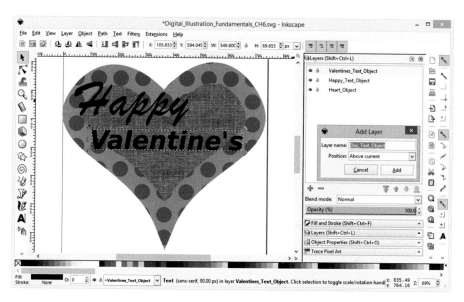

Figure 12-11. *Use Add Layer dialog to add Day_Text_Object layer*

The final layered composite can be seen in Figure 12-12.

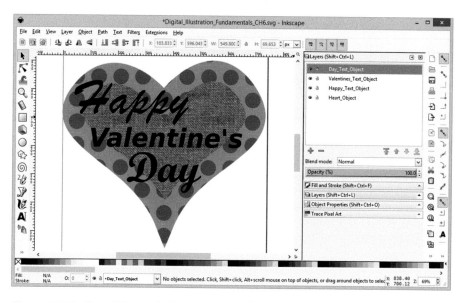

Figure 12-12. *Your Valentine's Day card project looks very nice*

It is important to notice that at the bottom of your Layers palette is an **Opacity** slider as well as a **Blend Mode** drop-down that will allow you to do the same kinds of special algorithmic compositing effects that you can do in GIMP, Photoshop, Painter 2016, PaintShop Pro, and Editshare Lightworks, among others.

Now let's look at some of the core layers and selection set (alpha channel) features for Corel Painter 2016. Since this is a fundamentals book, I can't really go into all the powerful layer features for this professional digital painting software package, but I can get you started with the features that you will use the most often with your digital painting compositing pipeline.

Painter Layers: Digital Paint Compositing

Let's open your Auto-Painting by using the **File ➤ Recent** menu sequence, shown at the left in Figure 12-13, and selecting the **Chapter-11-Auto-Paint.rif** option. As you can see, there are **Canvas** Layers and **RGB** Channels selected in floating palettes.

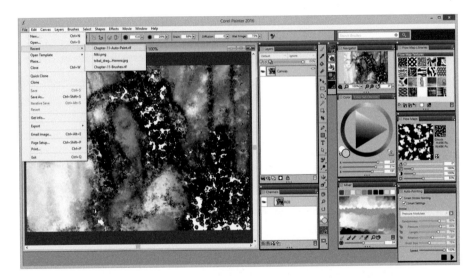

Figure 12-13. *Ensure Brush Pack you installed is on Brush menu*

The first thing I'm going to show you is the **Layers** menu and how to add a New Layer by using the **Layers ➤ New Layer** menu sequence, shown in Figure 12-14. There is an icon at the bottom of the Layers palette that looks like two pieces of paper. This will also create a New Layer with a single click from a stylus.

Figure 12-14. *Create a New Layer using a Layer ➤ New Layer menu*

Let's composite a ring element over the digital painting you created in Chapter 11. Use the **File ➤ Open** menu sequence as shown in Figure 12-15 and open the **RingElement.png** PNG32 image. You can see the new **Layer 1** layer you created selected in green on the right side of the digital painting in the Layers palette, and any new painting that you do will be on this new layer.

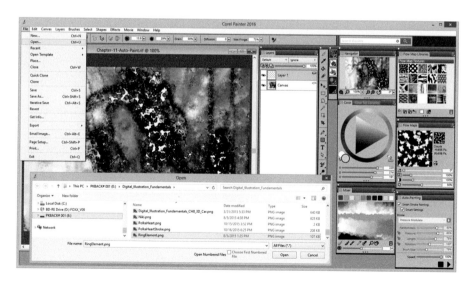

Figure 12-15. *Use File ➤ Open menu sequence to open RingElement*

Use the alpha channel (selection set) to select only the RingElement by using the
Select ➤ Load Selection menu sequence, and **Load From Layer 1 Transparency** and
Replace Selection in the **Load Selection** dialog, shown in Figure 12-16, on the left side.

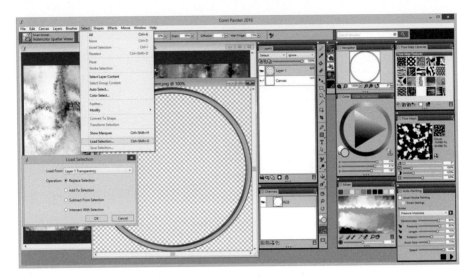

Figure 12-16. *Select the RingElement using its alpha channel*

Use the **Edit ➤ Paste** menu sequence shown in Figure 12-17 to add this RingElement
over the top of your digital painting.

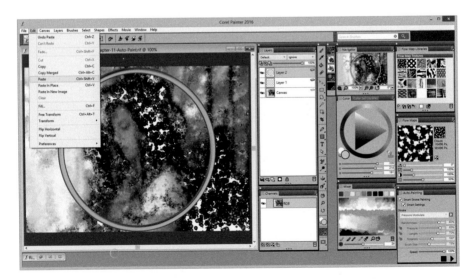

Figure 12-17. *Paste the selected RingElement into your painting*

Select the Magic Wand tool, shown on the right in Figure 12-18, and select **Layer 2** and click in the middle to select the inside of the RingElement. Use a **Select ➤ Invert Selection** menu sequence to invert the selection, and select the outside of the Ring so that we can delete everything except what is inside it.

Figure 12-18. *Invert selection, using Select ➤ Invert Selection*

Since layer operations are "modal," click on your **Canvas** layer to select it, before using your **Delete** key. This removes digital painting data outside your ring, shown in Figure 12-19.

Figure 12-19. *Your final composite is a painting inside a Ring*

As you can see, using layers and alpha channels give you a big boost in productivity and flexibility in creating artwork in any genre of digital new media content production tools; in the case of this book this is digital illustration and digital painting software packages. These same exact concepts and work processes apply for digital image compositing and digital video editing software package as well.

Summary

In this twelfth chapter, we took a closer look at layers and channels and how they are used to create more complex digital projects and to manage objects and their selection sets. I did this so that over the next couple of advanced chapters, covering things such as **programming** and **publishing**, you would have some of the knowledge that I cover in my *Digital Image Compositing Fundamentals* title (Apress, 2015), which is important to understand if you are creating applications, eBooks, or web sites and similar new media digital projects. We will look at programming languages in greater detail during Chapter 13, so you will need this advanced knowledge soon.

CHAPTER 13

∎∎∎

The Automation of Digital Illustration: Programming

Now that you have learned how to create professional digital illustrations, using powerful features in digital illustration and digital painting software packages, exporting SVG or PNG to the most popular and widespread vector and raster file formats used in the most popular programming platforms, it's time to take a look at those programming platforms themselves, just in case you want to take your digital illustration and digital painting compositing career to the next level.

During this chapter you'll learn about delivering digital illustration (SVG) and digital painting (PNG) content using the popular open source programming languages that support digital imaging (PNG) and digital illustration (SVG) such as Java, CSS3, and HTML5, JavaFX, JavaScript, and XML for content delivery via Android Studio, iOS, Blackberry OS, Tizen OS, Mozilla's Firefox OS, Opera OS, and Google's Chrome OS (also known as Chromium).

This is important information to know if you plan to use digital illustration or digital paintings created by using the concepts and work processes covered in this book in programming projects, using **open software development platforms**, or, if you have an interest in learning more about adding programming into your vast digital content production and publishing repertoire.

The platforms run a majority of the Consumer Electronics Industry hardware devices, and include **Java** (Android Studio and WebKit), **JavaFX** (Android, iOS, Windows, Linux, MacOSX, Solaris), and **JavaScript** with CSS3 and HTML5 scripting (WebKit Browsers).

This chapter is not going to teach you programming, for that would take a number of books (and coding experience), but it will expose you to what's possible if you extend the journey you're on from digital illustration and digital painting to new media software development. Everything that we will be covering in the chapter is free for commercial use! You can download XML and HTML5 (NetBeans 8.1), Android Studio (IntelliJ), Java 8 and JavaFX, as well as JavaScript; they are also included with NetBeans.

Normally, I would start the chapter covering an internal scripting language such as the GIMP ScriptFu (please don't ask) or Photoshop ExtendScript, but we have already covered SVG XML, and Painter 2016 does not have any internal scripting language, so let's get right into what I will call "external" programming languages. Let's start off with the most widespread application development language, Java 8; and its JavaFX APIs, which can be used for Android OS, iOS, Windows, Macintosh, Linux, and Solaris Applications development, as well as in web sites or appliances.

© Wallace Jackson 2015
W. Jackson, *Digital Illustration Fundamentals*, DOI 10.1007/978-1-4842-1697-2_13

Java and JavaFX: javafx.scene.effect API

Digital illustration and digital painting compositing pipelines can be built and controlled using code in the Java programming language, as can be seen in Figure 13-1. The backplate imagery is a PNG24, the 3D logo is a PNG32, and the script text images are PNG32 as well. The text is vector artwork and could contain SVG objects created in Inkscape as well using the same code. Java has a library called **JavaFX**, which provides expansive new media asset support spanning digital illustration (SVG) and digital painting (PNG), as well as digital imaging, digital audio, digital video, and i3D real-time OpenGL rendering. Most of the digital illustration data, filters and XML we have been using during this book are in the **javafx.scene.shape** library and the **javafx.scene.effects** library. JavaFX 8 applications run in HTML5, Android, or iOS; thus Java, the world's most popular programming language, is truly "code once, deliver everywhere."

The splashscreen for a game I am coding, for my upcoming Pro Java Games Development title (Apress, 2016), can be seen in Figure 13-1. The upper-left quadrant is the splashscreen itself and uses a PNG24 backplate image overlayed with PNG23 composite images (two), vector (text) elements, and user interface button elements. Since digital painting assets should be PNG24 you can simply substitute your digital painting assets for the rendered 3D assets shown as the background imagery here for your digital illustration and digital painting workflow, using the same file formats that I use here, and the exact same Java 8 and JavaFX 8 programing logic.

Figure 13-1. *Compositing raster and vector assets usingJavaFX*

As you can see, the quality level afforded by Java 8 and JavaFX 8 is amazing and available for playback on nearly every popular platform, including Android, iOS, Blackberry, FireFox, Opera, Chrome, Windows, Linux, Solaris, and Macintosh OS X.

The Java and JavaFX code can be seen in Figure 13-2. The JavaFX API is part of the Java API; thus, JavaFX is Java. These were separate programming languages until JavaFX was acquired by Sun Microsystems, right before Sun was acquired by Oracle.

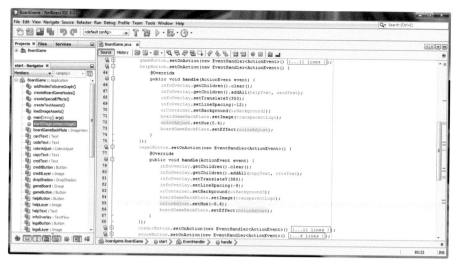

Figure 13-2. *JavaFX code adds raster and vector assets to game*

I show the code for two of the buttons, the **Instructions** and the **Copyrights** button, called **helpButton** and **legalButton** in the Java code, shown in Figure 13-2. I do not seek to teach you coding during this chapter; however Java code is understandable enough to explain to you what is going on for this compositing.

The boardGameBackPlate.setImage(transparentLogo); Java statement is changing my digital image asset in my backplate layer, using terms that you are now familiar with from this book.

The colorAdjust.setHue(0.4); Java statement color shifts the logo 40% (you color shifted 140%, achieving cyan to wine color) around the color wheel, and the colorAdjust.setHue(-0.4); Java code color shifts the logo 40% around the color wheel in an opposite direction. With a color slider it would be 40% to the right and 40% to the left, respectively.

Vertical, Y axis pixel positioning is being accomplished using the infoOverlay.setTranslateY(350); Java code and text spacing is being accomplished using an infoOverlay.setLineSpacing(-12); Java statement. This is how an image composite is created with code!

Next, let's take a look at image compositing pipelines, implemented using only basic markup languages (HTML5 and CSS3).

HTML5 and CSS3: Markup Compositing

Whereas Java (JavaFX) is the most popular programming language, HTML5 and CSS3 markup languages are the most widespread as far as usage is concerned. This is because they are used in every browser, which all use an API called **WebKit**, as does Android and iOS, so they are used in these OSes as well. There are also several HTML5 OSes out now, not surprisingly, from the makers of the HTML5 browsers. These include Chrome

OS, Firefox OS, and Opera OS. These are used in Smartphones, Tablets, and iTV Sets. For instance, Panasonic iTV sets use Firefox OS, Sony Bravia uses Opera OS, Google has a range of Chrome hardware products, and Alcatel uses Firefox OS for its Smartphone internationally.

I composited the HDTV resolution www.iTVset.com web site, using only lossless codecs and with a combination of **PNG24**, **SVG**, and **aniGIF** for backplate sections, as well as **PNG32** for all i3D UI element overlays. As you can see in Figure 13-3, the entire site looks like an uncompressed true color BMP image, however it is animated using JavaScript and is also fully interactive. The site was coded in only 24 lines of HTML5, and less than 2MB for total graphic image asset data footprint overhead. This is made possible by a digital compositing (layer) pipeline allowing the "granularization" of the digital assets, which allows me to use far smaller asset file sizes, which results in faster transfer.

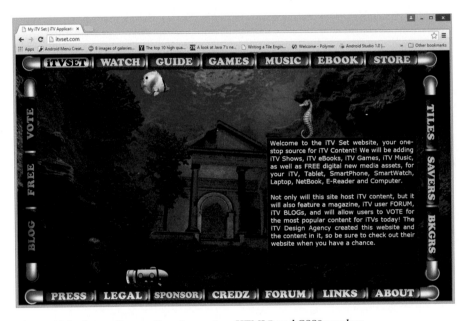

Figure 13-3. *Image Composite using custom HTML5 and CSS3 markup*

Additionally, a lot of **indexed color** assets can be used, allowing a site that looks like it is true color but in fact is not. For instance, all six animated elements on the page use an indexed color **animGIF** file format with the 1-bit pre-multiplied alpha channel (uses average background color to hide aliasing).

The i3D user interface button elements use **PNG32** format, using its **alpha channel** to composite the UI seamlessly over any background image used in any section of this web site, including digital video, Java (JavaFX) applications, 3D animation as seen on the www.iTVSet.com home page, or full screen imagery.

Graphics elements are held in HTML5 **<DIV>** tags, and CSS3 is used for **blending**, **opacity**, **positioning**, and **interactivity**. I do not obstruct the right-click action with my code in any way, so you can right-click on the site and "View as Source" to look at any of this code, at any time during the site's development.

Text is rendered by WebKit in its own <DIV> tag regions, using HTML5 to define content and metatag and styled with CSS3.

As you can see, just like Java and JavaFX, HTML5 and CSS can provide you with a vector compositing pipeline that can be almost as powerful as GIMP and Photoshop. However you will have to be a creative and a savvy programmer in order to pull these capabilities out of open source SVG, HTML5, CSS, and JavaScript.

Android Studio: Using a PorterDuff Object

The Google Android OS platform is running more Smartphones, eBook eReaders, Tablets, iTV Sets, Game Consoles, Smartwatches, and IoT devices than any other OS platform in the world. In fact, I have written a series of **Pro Android** titles for Apress from 2013 through 2016, including *Pro Android Graphics* (2013), *Pro Android UI* (2014), *Pro Android Wearables* (2015), and I am currently writing *Pro Android IoT* (2016). I cover how to code for the **PorterDuff** pixel blending and pixel transfer modes in the *Pro Android Graphics* title, and in fact, Figure 13-4 shows one of the screenshots from this book, showing three different blend modes in use in the Nexus One Emulator in the Eclipse IDE. You've seen these blending modes in your Layers palette in Chapter 12 in GIMP 2.8, Inkscape, as well as in Painter 2016.

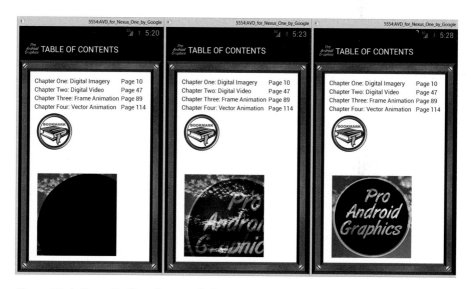

Figure 13-4. *PorterDuff mode example from Pro Android Graphics*

The Java code to put together this compositing pipeline, which has a PNG24 backplate, PNG32 ring element, PNG32 3D logo, and alpha controlled vector, with a black fill color, is quite complex, as can be seen in Figure 13-5. I will go through what these statements do so you can see a compositing code pipeline that matches up with that layer-based compositing pipeline that you have become familiar with during the previous Chapter (12).

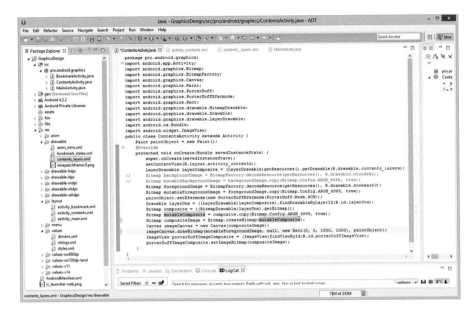

Figure 13-5. *Java code for implementing a compositing pipeline*

Layers are called **LayerDrawable** in Android, so the first line of code loads the LayerDrawable with a **contents_layers.png** asset using a getResources().getDrawable() method call "chain."

I commented out a backgroundImage plate, for testing, so I will just cover the foregroundImage plate code here. I create a Bitmap object named **foregroundImage** and load it with an asset named **cloudsky.png** with a **BitmapFactory.decodeResource()** method call. I make that Bitmap object mutable (changeable) by putting it into memory using a **.copy()** method call specifying the **8-bit ARGB** color depth (this is also called the 32-bit color space).

I then set a PorterDuff **transfer mode** (sometimes called a **blending mode**, although technically some blending modes will transfer pixels rather than blending them together) on a Paint object using the .setXfermode() method, using the XOR mode.

I create a Drawable object, named **layerOne**, and load it, with a Bitmap object named **composite**, and load that into memory as a mutableComposite, and using that, I create a Bitmap object named **compositeImage**. I then create a Canvas object to draw on, named **imageCanvas** and load that with the compositeImage object.

Next I draw the Bitmap object on the Canvas object using the **imageCanvas. drawBitmap()** method call that specifies an area using a square 1,000 pixel **Rect** object, the blending mode using the **paintObject** and a **mutableForegroundImage** as a Bitmap object (bitmap or raster image that I specified as 32-bit ARGB_8888).

I create an **ImageView** named **porterDuffImageComposite**, to hold (display) this pipeline in my user interface design, and I load this ImageView by using the **.setImageBitmap()** method call.

Game Design: SVG for Collision Detection

Let's take a look at how I use SVG data for a **collision polygon** in my *Beginning Java 8 Game Design* title from Apress. As you'll see in Figure 13-6, I use the **Pen Path Tool** in GIMP, to create a low-data (only 15 data points to process) collision cage for my invinciBagel character's sprite (one of the run cycle cels is seen here). GIMP 2.8 can save out SVG XML data as well!

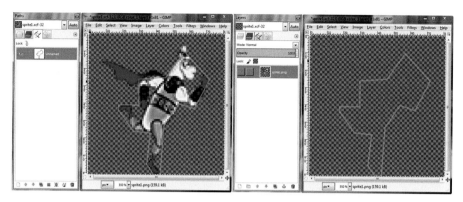

Figure 13-6. *SVG data used for a game sprite collision polygon*

Figure 13-7 shows my raw SVG XML data exported from GIMP before I optimize it using the exact same work process I showed you in this book, using SVG XML data exported using Inkscape.

```
sprite1svghand - Notepad
File  Edit  Format  View  Help
<?xml version="1.0" encoding="UTF-8" standalone="no"?>
<!DOCTYPE svg PUBLIC "-//W3C//DTD SVG 20010904//EN"
"http://www.w3.org/TR/2001/REC-SVG-20010904/DTD/svg10.dtd">
<svg xmlns="http://www.w3.org/2000/svg" width="1.125in" height="1.125in" viewBox="0 0 81 81">
    <path id="Unnamed" fill="none" stroke="black" stroke-width="1"
          d="M 56.73,10.00
             C 56.73,10.00 45.82,25.09 45.82,25.09
               45.82,25.09 30.18,26.36 30.18,26.36
               30.18,26.36 30.00,40.55 30.00,40.55
               30.00,40.55 18.00,40.73 18.00,40.73
               18.00,40.73 17.82,44.36 17.82,44.36
               17.82,44.36 26.91,56.00 26.91,56.00
               26.91,56.00 37.45,56.73 37.45,56.73
               37.45,56.73 34.91,74.91 34.91,74.91
               34.91,74.91 38.55,80.91 38.55,80.91
               38.55,80.91 42.73,80.73 42.73,80.73
               42.73,80.73 44.91,52.91 44.91,52.91
               44.91,52.91 53.82,40.18 53.82,40.18
               53.82,40.18 62.91,42.55 62.91,42.55
               62.91,42.55 72.36,26.36 72.36,26.36 Z" /> </svg>
```

Figure 13-7. *SVG XML data from Pen Tool path exported from GIMP*

As you will see in Figure 13-8, I reduced the coordinate pairs from 45 to 15, or about a **300%** data footprint reduction!

155

Figure 13-8. *Optimize SVG Command String data; select for Java*

I copied this data into an Array object in Java as a subobject called **spriteFrame** in my **iBagel** object, so, to reference this data I use iBagel.spriteFrame; and to access the **invinciBagel** class (an even larger object), I use invinciBagel.iBagel.spriteFrame, as can be seen in green, on Java code line **122** in Figure 13-9.

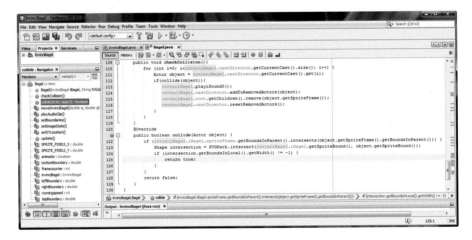

Figure 13-9. *Collision detection Java code referencing SVG data*

As you can see, all the concepts that I have covered over the course of the book are usable in Java. You can bet that all of these concepts are supported in each of these major platform (Java, JavaFX, HTML5, CSS3, JavaScript, Android) areas, which I have covered in the chapter. The reason for this is because the platforms are open source, as are the PorterDuff modes, OpenGL, JPG, SVG, GIF, PNG, XML, 3D, alpha channels, GIMP, and Inkscape.

As you can see in Figure 13-10, Java or JavaFX allow you to create some pretty impressive multimedia productions, using digital illustration data, in SVG command formats, and digital painting data in PNG24 format.

Figure 13-10. *JavaFX game using digital illustration, SVG and image compositing*

Since all of the areas of digital asset compositing will be "free for commercial use," it is logical for the open source platforms to completely incorporate them. All this is excellent news for digital image compositing aficionados, to be sure!

Summary

In this thirteenth chapter, you learned about advanced topics that relate to computer programming, and how different programming languages can support the digital asset compositing endeavors, either inside digital asset compositing software, as a work process, or SVG special effects plug-ins, or SVG XML markup, or outside your digital asset compositing software, for taking your creation to the next level, by adding interactivity and other useful features, limited only by your imagination.

First you looked at several popular open source platform programming languages and how these can be utilized to create the same digital asset compositing effects that you can create using Inkscape, GIMP, and Painter 2016, all of which are covered in this book.

Next, you looked at Java and its JavaFX new media engine and saw how that platform supports digital asset compositing as well as advanced blending modes and special effects algorithms.

Then you looked at HTML5 and CSS3 and saw this platform could also implement the digital asset compositing concepts and techniques you learned in this book using only markup languages for deliverables such as web sites and HTML5 OS applications.

Finally you looked at using SVG Command data in JavaFX 8 games to create "collision detection polygons" that are highly optimized for using low amounts of system memory. You looked at the PorterDuff class, and some advanced Java code, showing that a compositing pipeline with blending modes can be coded in Java and JavaFX or used in Android Studio for advanced digital image compositing savvy applications. JavaFX apps also work in iOS.

In the next chapter, we will take a look at some popular content publishing platforms and device types.

CHAPTER 14

■ ■ ■

Publish Digital Illustration: Content Delivery Platforms

Now that you have an understanding of the fundamental concepts, terms, and principles in digital illustration, digital painting, digital compositing, and programming, it is time to look at how digital illustration content can be **published** with popular open source publishing platforms. I'm going to delineate the chapter based on **consumer electronics hardware device genres**, as these define the different types of applications. For instance, **eBook eReaders**, such as Amazon's Kindle Fire, use Kindle KF8 format; **Smartwatches** use Android Wear SDK under the Android Studio 1.4, using the Android OS 5.4 API; **iTV Sets** use the **Android TV** SDK in Android Studio 1.4, using the Android OS 5.4 API, **Automobile Dashboards** use **Android Auto** SDK with the Android Studio 1.4 IDE with the Android OS 5.4 API; **Tablets** and **SmartPhones** use Android SDK in Android Studio 1.4 IDE with the Android OS 5.4 API; **Laptops** and **NetBooks** use Java with JavaFX; and each of these hardware devices also support all of the open industry publishing standards, such as PDF, HTML5, and EPUB3.

We'll continue to look at how to publish with electronic hardware device types, using the software development platforms that these devices support, such as Kindle KF8, EPUB3, Android Studio 1.4 (Android OS 5.4), Java, JavaFX, PDF, HTML5, CSS3, and JavaScript, some of which we already covered in Chapter 13.

Open Source Formats: PDF, HTML, EPUB

Let's start with the content publishing formats that support digital illustration that have been defined by industry groups, as **EPUB** and **HTML** have, or which have been "open sourced" as the Adobe **Portable Document Format**, or **PDF**, has been. Each of these formats supports the SVG digital illustration format, as you will see during this section of the chapter. I am starting with these open formats, as they are usable across every type of hardware device so I'll start with platforms with wide support.

© Wallace Jackson 2015
W. Jackson, *Digital Illustration Fundamentals*, DOI 10.1007/978-1-4842-1697-2_14

Portable Document Format: Digital Illustration PDF

The Adobe PDF Portable Document format is utilized by the Adobe **Acrobat Reader**, used around the world for publishing rich media documents that can include **digital illustration**, digital audio, digital video, digital images, or i3D (interactive 3D). Acrobat Reader is free and its **PDF** format has been open sourced. The **Adobe Acrobat Professional** series of publishing tools are still paid software packages and well worth the money, if you need to publish via this widely accepted rich media document publishing format. This PDF format supports two digital illustration formats, **EPS** and **PostScript**, the best option being EPS, as far as your quality to file size ratio is concerned. This is because the PDF file format will keep the vector data intact and render it at whatever screen size is being used. You can also use Inkscape to export to EPS, PostScript, and even to PDF directly, so you don't need PDF to support SVG directly, which it does not, probably because it is a competing vector format.

It used to be a PDF was only used for creating business documents. However, it has been adopted for an eBook format; in fact, you might be reading my books using the PDF format. Other eBook formats include Kindle (.MOBI) and EPUB (EPUB3), which we will be covering later on during this chapter as well.

Another advantage of this PDF document publishing format is that it offers **Digital Rights Management** (DRM) support. This allows you to copy protect (lock) your document, if you want to sell it for money. Adobe has a PDF Server product incorporating this DRM feature that allows you to better market PDF content.

It is rumored that the other two publishing formats that we are covering in this section of the chapter are also looking at adding DRM support in the future. Let's look at HTML5 next.

HyperText Markup Language: HTML5 Digital Audio

You've already taken a look at how to use SVG and PNG formats in Chapter 13, and thus you know HTML5 supports the SVG digital illustration format, as well as the **PNG8, PNG24, PNG32, JPEG, GIF,** and **AnimGIF** digital painting imagery file formats.

It used to be that HTML5 was only used for creating your web site designs, until the web browser manufacturers decided to utilize their web browser code to create **HTML5 OSs** for consumer electronics devices given the success of Android, Bada, and iOS.

Putting this browser code, with **app launch icon** support, on top of the **Linux OS Kernel**, produced a **Chrome OS** (Motorola), **Firefox OS** (Panasonic iTV), and **Opera OS** (Sony Bravia iTV Sets).

There's also **Tizen OS** (Samsung), which is managed by The Linux Foundation for the creator of the Linux OS Linus Torvald.

Tizen also uses HTML5. HTML5 is easy to implement, thanks to your open source **WebKit API**, which is also a part of Android Studio 1.4 (Android OS 5.4, and now Android 6.0).

HTML5 application and web site publishing is therefore an excellent way to deliver content across all embedded mobile OS, desktop OS, and web browser platforms. This is why DRM is in the future of HTML5, and why I showed you how to implement digital painting assets by using HTML5 and CSS3 in Chapter 13.

Next, let's take a closer look at the open source EPUB 3 publishing standard, used for eBooks, and soon for much more.

Electronic Publishing: Digital Audio in EPUB3

The EPUB specification is a distribution and interchange format standard for digital publications and documents. EPUB 3, the third major release of the open EPUB standard, consists of four specifications, each defining an important component of an overall EPUB document. **EPUB Publications 3** defines publication-level semantics, as well as conformance requirements for EPUB 3 documents. **EPUB Content Documents 3** defines XHTML, SVG and CSS3 profiles for use in the context of your EPUB 3.0 publications. **EPUB Open Container Format 3.0**, or OCF3, defines a file format, as well as a processing model for encapsulating sets of related resource assets in one single ZIP file format (EPUB Container). **EPUB Media Overlays 3.0** defines a format and a processing model for the data synchronization of text with digital audio assets.

EPUB 3.0 has been widely adopted as a format for digital books, also popularly known as "eBooks." This 3.0 specification significantly increases the EPUB format's capability, so that it would be capable of supporting a range of new media publication requirements. These would include complex layout, new media and interactivity, and international typography (fonts) support.

The hope is that EPUB 3 will be utilized for a broad range of content, including books; magazines; and educational, professional, and scientific publications.

EPUB 3 supports SVG digital illustration embedded in the document using SVG, and digital painting using PNG, JPEG, or GIF formats. These would inherit the same functions and feature set that these formats provide in HTML5.

Another impressive new media feature in EPUB 3 is called **Media Overlay Documents**. Media Overlay Documents could be used with SVG documents, such as those we created during this book. Media Overlay Documents also provide the ability to synchronize your digital audio assets with vector elements inside the Publishing Content Document (EPUB3 publishing platforms), which could be used for some very powerful presentation capabilities.

Open Platforms: Java, Android, and Kindle

The next set of formats I am going to cover are open source and free for commercial use, but do not run across every hardware device, and are not industry specifications, but instead are owned by major industry hardware and software manufacturers. Oracle owns Java and JavaFX, Google owns Android, and Amazon owns Kindle (.MOBI) and Kindle Fire, which uses the KF8 format. Let's cover these based on the genres or types of consumer electronics devices that these run on, starting with eBook Readers, since the three formats we just covered are all widely used for delivering eBooks as well, as you can see on the Apress.com web site, when you purchase your educational titles.

eBook Readers: Kindle Fire, Android, Java, or PDF

The eBook Reader hardware device is actually an Android tablet, which is why I added Android into the title for this section of the chapter. The world's most popular eBook Reader, Kindle Fire, runs Android OS, as does the Sony eBook Reader, and the Barnes and Noble NOOK eBook Reader. Even Apple iPad runs Kindle, EPUB3, and PDF eBook titles, as do Blackberry tablets, and Microsoft Surface tablets. The reason I added Java in the title for this section is that Kindle has Java capabilities for interactive eBooks, and Android uses Java as well. Since eBook readers will also read .PDF files, I also added PDF into this title.

Since most eBook Readers are actually Android tablets or iPads, there are a plethora of platforms, the key open ones you looked at (Chapter 13) for delivering SVG illustration content.

This means you will deliver digital illustration content user experiences with Android applications, HTML5 applications, Java applications, HTML5 web sites, Kindle eBooks, EPUB3 eBooks, NOOK eBooks, or interactive new media PDF documents. This gives you a ton of flexibility for publishing SVG with eBook Readers.

Since this would all be done using Java, JavaFX, Android Studio, HTML5, and SVG, the basics regarding how all this should be accomplished was covered during Chapters 7 and 13.

iTV Sets: Android TV, Java, JavaScript, and HTML5

The **iTV Set**, or interactive television set, is the most recent consumer electronics device to hit the marketplace, and iTV Set devices are expected to explode in sales during 2016 and 2017. This is the reason Google has developed a specialized version of Android SDK (Software Development Kit) for iTV Sets, called **Android TV API** (Application Programming Interface).

There are **HTML5 OS iTV Set** products as well from Samsung (Tizen OS), Panasonic (Firefox OS), and Sony (Opera OS), so the iTV Set consumer electronic device is much like an eBook Reader device, in that it will allow you to create and deliver digital audio content by using **Java** or **JavaFX** (Android OS or HTML5 OS), **HTML5** markup, **CSS3** and **JavaScript** (iOS, Android OS, HTML5 OS).

It's also important to realize that with iTV Set devices your viewers are going to be paying closer attention to content streams, including digital illustration, digital painting, i3D, and digital imagery, digital audio, and digital video.

The viewer paying close attention to your content is not always the case with devices such as Smartphones, or automobile dashboards (at least, let's hope not).

If you want to deliver digital audio content across each of these iTV Set device platforms, you would use HTML5. Android and iOS support HTML5, but HTML5 OS and web sites do not support Android and iOS applications. The other side of the decision is that Apple and Google Play have more advanced app stores, so if you are going to monetize your digital illustration and digital painting content, you would be considering developing apps with Java (Android) or JavaFX (iOS) more than using JavaScript under HTML5 OSes or HTML5 browsers, although these fully support SVG.

Smartwatches: Android WEAR, Java, and HTML5

The **Smartwatch** is the next most recent consumer electronics device genre to hit the market. The Smartwatch devices are also expected to explode in sales during 2016 and 2017, primarily because there are hundreds of manufacturers manufacturing them. This is because the densely populated watch industry is moving to release smartwatch products, so that they do not lose market share to consumer electronics manufacturers, such as LGE, Sony, Motorola, and Samsung, who already have several smartwatch products each. One of the first custom Android APIs that Google ever developed was **Android WEAR** along with its **Watch Faces API**.

Digital Illustration is an important feature that these smartwatch devices are going to support, because vector formats are highly optimized, from a data footprint standpoint, and SVG rendering support is built into Android Wear hardware devices.

What this means is that a smartwatch product is like an animated digital illustration time piece for your user's wrist! It can provide professional digital illustration asset playback results with overlayed smartwatch functionality.

This is significant for digital illustration producer or digital painting application developer professionals, which is why I'm including it as part of this digital illustration book.

Another important feature of smartwatches is that you'll be able to combine your digital audio assets with other highly functional attributes, such as time, date, weather, fashion, and health features popular with smartwatches, such as fitness and physical health monitoring (heart, pulse, etc.) hardware input.

Once smartwatch screen resolutions go up from 320 pixels to 480, 640, or 800 pixels, even more functionality would become available to developers. The Huawei smartwatch already features a 400 x 400 pixel screen, so, high resolution smartwatches should be appearing during 2016 or 2017 given that smartphones have 4K screens that are only 5 to 7 inches, so an 800 pixel smartwatch screen is certainly possible, as the technology exists already.

So as long as your smartwatch user has quality bluetooth headphones and you process and then optimize your 16-bit 48 kHz digital audio assets perfectly, and use the lossless FLAC codec or high-quality settings for the OggVorbis or MPEG-4 AAC codec, you should have your smartwatch users rocking their socks off!

Auto Dashboards: Android AUTO, Java, and HTML5

The **Automobile Dashboard** is the next most recent consumer electronics device genre to hit the mass market. Auto dashboard devices are expected to become standard in cars by 2016 or 2017 as a number of manufacturers already have them as standard equipment, and all of the automobile manufacturers have signed on with Google to support Android AUTO, the custom Android SDK for automobile dashboard applications. Automobiles are another hyper-competitive industry not likely to get left behind as far as technology is concerned, so this is another logical market for Android and HTML5 OSes to get into.

Digital audio is again a very important feature for auto dashboards to support, because extensive (and expensive) ultra-high-quality audio playback hardware is often built right into the body of an automobile, especially in more expensive brands, which are almost half of the automobile brands in the market.

Digital audio is also the best fit for Android AUTO apps because there are stringent guidelines regarding tasking driver attention off of the road, and digital audio Android AUTO apps do not require the user to look at any display screen, and are thus the safest type of Android AUTO apps and will pass muster in the Google Play Automotive App section of the online store.

As you've seen in the last three sections of the chapter, there are several entirely new consumer electronic device types that have essentially zero apps, especially digital audio apps that have been developed for them, so the opportunity for audio developers is nothing short of immense – so make some big money!

SmartPhone and Tablet: Android, Java, and HTML5

Smartphones or **tablets** have been around the longest, as has the hybrid between the two, commonly referred to as a **phablet**. The Android OS covers all of these device types as well as personal computers that run the Android OS. There are currently billions of smartphones, as well as billions of tablets, and almost 100 major consumer electronics manufacturers that have made products for the open source Android operating system platform. For this reason, this is a significant opportunity for digital illustration content and applications, as there are not as many of these digital illustration or digital painting applications as there are video, audio, or image (photographic) applications.

All your popular smartphones and tablets include support for your SVG command data, and SVG XML file formats, as well as for rendering vector illustration data into raster imagery data that fits user's device screen displays with a pixel-for-pixel precision. This results in high-quality content consumption.

Game Console: Android, Java, JavaFX, and HTML5

Since Android, Java, JavaFX, and HTML5 now support **OpenGL ES 3.1** a plethora of advanced game console products have appeared that are affordable priced between $50 and $100. This is yet another opportunity waiting to happen for digital illustrations gurus, which you'll soon be, once you practice what you learned in the book. These consoles run Android and therefore support Java and HTML5, as well as JavaFX apps or Android applications, and even eBooks, for that matter. There are over a dozen brands out now.

Some major industry brands (manufacturers) are producing game controllers with Android computers inside, for instance, an nVidia Shield, or GameStick. Other major manufacturers, such as Amazon, manufacture a game console iTV Set hybrid product, such as the Amazon Fire TV. Others such as OUYA and GamePop make STB (Set Top Box) products that game controllers (and iTV Set) will plug into. Some, such as OUYA and Razer ForgeTV, come with both the STB and the Game Controller, for a complete gaming package.

Since all these support Android, you can utilize vectors via SVGXML formats and SVG commands covered in this book, and if you use HTML5 or EPUB3 you can use SVG commands, SVG filters or SVG XML. I covered the code for doing this in Chapter 7.

SVG data can also be used inside of the OpenGL Rendering Engine that runs many of the games, for texture mapping, as can digital painting assets. Texture maps are applied as "skins" to 3D "mesh" geometry, so 3D can take your digital illustration or digital painting content production pipelines to all new levels using open source 3D software packages such as Blender. You can download **Blender 2.76** for free, at http://www.blender.org today!

Future Devices: Robots, VR, and Home Appliances

The future of Android SDKs will surely bring more custom APIs. I expect to see an **Android VR**, for virtual reality goggles, as well as **Android HOME** for home appliances or home control units, and maybe even an **Android ROBOT** SDK for Android-based robots. I have already seen many of these products in the marketplace for some time so it's up to Google to provide custom APIs for these product genres, all of which will be great digital illustration applications, and great digital painting application platforms, for digital illustrators and digital painters as well as for multimedia producers and application developers who are digital illustrators and digital painters.

Digital illustration as well as digital painting will be an important component in all these emerging device genres. I'd expect at least two of these genres, Home Appliances and VR, to showcase interactive digital painting as a way to increase user experience levels (VR), and because UHD home theaters have the full attention of the viewers.

Paid Software Platforms: iOS or Windows

The last section will cover formats which are not open source, that is, they involve paid software, and, in the case of Apple Computer, paid hardware, which will be required to develop for these platforms. Some of these require the company who owns the platform to approve (allow) your software before it can be sold in the application store. It is important to note that you will be able to get around this approval process by developing using HTML5 for these platforms, or using JavaFX; therefore you could still deliver content for your clients without having to invest thousands in hardware (for iOS) and in software (Windows Visual C++ or C# software development packages).

Apple iPhone and iPad: Supported Audio Formats

As a proprietary format, Apple and iOS do not directly support SVG as all of the other platforms and devices in the world do. There are some third-party solutions and work-arounds to this, like the SVGKit project on GitHub (`https://github.com/SVGKit/SVGKit`).

This is why I have focused primarily on the open source operating systems and publishing platforms in this book that do support digital illustration and digital painting formats, such as SVG and PNG, currently in use in Java, JavaFX, Android Studio, and HTML5.

Windows Phone: Supported Digital Audio Formats

As a proprietary format, Windows and WindowsPhone also do not directly support SVG, as all of the other platforms and devices in the world do. SVG support was added in Internet Explorer 9, and there is an extension you can get for Microsoft Explorer to render SVG file thumbnails. As Microsoft and Apple represent an increasingly smaller operating system market share percentage as time goes on, and free open platforms continue to gain market share percentages, this will become less and less of an issue for digital illustrators.

Summary

In this final chapter we took a look at digital illustration and digital painting publishing concepts, principles, platforms, and file formats that you will use to compress and decompress your digital illustration and digital painting assets, as well as to publish and distribute these to your end users. We looked at many of the different formats, platforms, and devices that will be available to you for developing digital illustration and digital painting interactive new media content.

I hope you have enjoyed this journey through the digital illustration, digital painting, layer compositing, programming, and digital publishing concepts and work processes.

Now that you have a fundamental knowledge of digital illustration that you can build on in the future, for your new media design, multimedia development, and 2D content publishing endeavors, you can create the next big vector-based application or game that will captivate users in the marketplace.

Be sure to keep your eye out for my other books covering Android Studio, Java and JavaFX, HTML5, JSON, or other new media genres such as digital image compositing, digital audio editing, and digital painting techniques.

Index

© Wallace Jackson 2015
W. Jackson, *Digital Illustration Fundamentals*, DOI 10.1007/978-1-4842-1697-2